# Evaluating Public Research Institutions

*Evaluating Public Research Institutions* provides the first detailed case study analysis of what is arguably one of the United States' hallmark public sector research programs: the Advanced Technology Program (ATP). The ATP's primary objective is to assist US business in creating and applying new technologies in order to maintain a competitive edge in a rapidly changing world economy.

This book presents a unique, systematic study of a public agency's pioneering intramural research program and provides a methodological illustration of how other public organizations should proceed when conducting such an evaluation.

This book will be of great interest to academics and researchers in economics as well as policy makers who are involved in program evaluation.

**Albert N. Link** is Professor of Economics at the University of North Carolina at Greensboro, USA.

**John T. Scott** is Professor of Economics at Dartmouth College, USA.

## Studies in Global Competition Series

*A series of books edited by John Cantwell, The University of Reading, UK and David Mowery, University of California, Berkeley, USA*

**Volume 1**
**Japanese Firms in Europe**
*Edited by Frédérique Sachwald*

**Volume 2**
**Technological Innovation, Multinational Corporations and New International Competitiveness**
The case of intermediate countries
*Edited by José Molero*

**Volume 3**
**Global Competition and the Labour Market**
*By Nigel Driffield*

**Volume 4**
**The Source of Capital Goods Innovation**
The role of user firms in Japan and Korea
*By Kong-Rae Lee*

**Volume 5**
**Climates of Global Competition**
*By Maria Bengtsson*

**Volume 6**
**Multinational Enterprises and Technological Spillovers**
*By Tommaso Perez*

**Volume 7**
**Governance of International Strategic Alliances**
Technology and transaction costs
*By Joanne E. Oxley*

**Volume 8**
**Strategy in Emerging Markets**
Telecommunications establishments in Europe
*By Anders Pehrsson*

**Volume 9**
**Going Multinational**
The Korean experience of direct investment
*Edited by Frédérique Sachwald*

**Volume 10**
**Multinational Firms and Impacts on Employment, Trade and Technology**
New perspectives for a new century
*Edited by Robert E. Lipsey and Jean-Louis Mucchielli*

**Volume 11**
**Multinational Firms**
The global–local dilemma
*Edited by John H. Dunning and Jean-Louis Mucchielli*

**Volume 12**
**MIT and the Rise of**
**Entrepreneurial Science**
*Henry Etzkowitz*

**Volume 13**
**Technological Resources and**
**the Logic of Corporate**
**Diversification**
*Brian Silverman*

**Volume 14**
**The Economics of Innovation,**
**New Technologies and**
**Structural Change**
*Cristiano Antonelli*

**Volume 15**
**European Union Direct**
**Investment in China**
Characteristics, challenges and
perspectives
*Daniel Van Den Bulcke, Haiyan*
*Zhang and Maria do Céu Esteves*

**Volume 16**
**Biotechnology in Comparative**
**Perspective**
*Edited by Gerhard Fuchs*

**Volume 17**
**Technological Change and**
**Economic Performance**
*Albert N. Link and*
*Donald S. Siegel*

**Volume 18**
**Multinational Corporations and**
**European Regional Systems**
**of Innovation**
*John Cantwell and*
*Simona Iammarino*

**Volume 19**
**Knowledge and Innovation in**
**Regional Industry**
An entrepreneurial coalition
*Roel Rutten*

**Volume 20**
**Local Industrial Clusters**
Existence, emergence and
evolution
*Thomas Brenner*

**Volume 21**
**The Emerging Industrial**
**Structure of the Wider**
**Europe**
*Edited by Francis McGowen,*
*Slavo Radosevic and*
*Nick Von Tunzelmann*

**Volume 22**
**Entrepreneurship**
A new perspective
*Thomas Grebel*

**Volume 23**
**Evaluating Public Research**
**Institutions**
The US Advanced Technology
Program's intramural research
initiative
*Albert N. Link and*
*John T. Scott*

**Volume 24**
**Location and Competition**
*Edited by Steven Brakman and*
*Harry Garretsen*

# Evaluating Public Research Institutions

The US Advanced Technology Program's intramural research initiative

**Albert N. Link and John T. Scott**

Routledge
Taylor & Francis Group

LONDON AND NEW YORK

First published 2005
by Routledge
2 Park Square, Milton Park, Abingdon, Oxon OX14 4RN

Simultaneously published in the USA and Canada
by Routledge
270 Madison Ave, New York, NY 10016

*Routledge is an imprint of the Taylor & Francis Group*

Typeset in Times New Roman by
Newgen Imaging Systems (P) Ltd, Chennai, India
Printed and bound in Great Britain by
TJ International Ltd, Padstow, Cornwall, UK

*British Library Cataloguing in Publication Data*
A catalogue record for this book is available
from the British Library

*Library of Congress Cataloging in Publication Data*
A catalog record for this book has been requested

ISBN 0–415–70054–X

# Contents

*List of illustrations* ix
*Acknowledgments* xiii

1 Introduction 1

2 The role of public research institutions 10

3 Survey design and methodology 22

4 Quantitative analysis of the effects of ATP
intramural funding 27

5 Case study selection and methodology 63

6 Case study of wavelength references for
optical fiber communications 70

7 Case study of injectable composite bone grafts 81

8 Case study of Internet commerce for manufacturing 88

9 Case study of polymer composite dielectrics for
integrated thin-film capacitors 95

10 Alternative evaluation templates 103

*Notes* 106
*Bibliography* 117
*Index* 121

# Illustrations

## Figures

| | | |
|---|---|---|
| 1.1 | Allocation of intramural research funds, by FY | 4 |
| 1.2 | Allocation of intramural research funds, by laboratory | 5 |
| 2.1 | Spillover gap between social and private rates of return to R&D | 12 |
| 6.1 | Demand, unit cost, and net gain in producer and consumer surplus from the use of SRM 2517a | 79 |

## Tables

| | | |
|---|---|---|
| 1.1 | Intramural research funding as percentage of ATP allocations | 4 |
| 1.2 | Allocation of intramural research funds, by laboratory and by year | 6 |
| 1.3 | Allocation of intramural research funds, by laboratory | 7 |
| 2.1 | Factors creating barriers to innovation and technology | 16 |
| 3.1 | Survey instrument for NIST PIs | 22 |
| 4.1 | PI response rates to the survey, by laboratory | 29 |
| 4.2 | Project response rates to the survey, by laboratory | 29 |
| 4.3 | Project response rates to the survey, by year of origination | 30 |
| 4.4 | Effect of ATP intramural funding on the scope of laboratory research | 31 |
| 4.5 | Probit model of scope with sample selection | 32 |
| 4.6 | Predicted effect of ATP intramural funding on the scope of laboratory research | 33 |
| 4.7 | Publications per project resulting from ATP intramural projects | 34 |
| 4.8 | Probit model for response to the publication question | 35 |
| 4.9 | Negative binomial regression model for the number of publications from a project, with correction for sample selection | 36 |

4.10   Predicted publications per project resulting from ATP
        intramural projects                                          37
4.11   Citations per in-print publication resulting from ATP
        intramural projects                                          38
4.12   Negative binomial regression model for the number of
        citations per project, with correction for sample selection  39
4.13   Predicted citations per predicted publication from ATP
        intramural projects, with correction for selection, for the
        133 projects reporting at least one publication              40
4.14   Patents per project from the ATP intramural projects          40
4.15   Presentations per project resulting from ATP intramural
        projects                                                     40
4.16   Probit model of response to presentation question             41
4.17   Negative binomial regression model for the number of
        presentations per project, with correction for sample
        selection                                                    42
4.18   Predicted presentations per project resulting from ATP
        intramural projects                                          42
4.19   Impact of ATP intramural project on leveraging other
        sources of funding                                           43
4.20   Probit model of leveraging competency awards or similar
        funded awards with sample selection                          44
4.21   Comparison of publications for ATP intramural and NIST
        projects                                                     45
4.22   Probability of undertaking a similar research project absent
        ATP intramural funding                                       46
4.23   Probit model for undertaking similar project absent ATP
        funding with sample selection                                47
4.24   Predicted probability of undertaking a similar research
        project absent ATP intramural funding                        48
4.25   Effect of ATP intramural funding in achieving similar goals
        and milestones                                               48
4.26   Probit model with control for response for being ahead of
        schedule                                                     49
4.27   Predicted probability of being ahead of the hypothetical
        project                                                      50
4.28   Model for the number of months ahead of schedule             51
4.29   The predicted number of months ahead of schedule             52
4.30   Scope of ATP intramural project compared to the similar
        hypothetical project                                         52
4.31   Probit model for broader scope as compared with the
        hypothetical project and with control for response           53

4.32 The predicted probabilities of broader scope as compared
with the hypothetical project                                    54
4.33 Technical challenge of ATP intramural project compared
to the similar hypothetical project                              54
4.34 Probit model for the ATP project being more technically
challenging than the hypothetical project                        55
4.35 The predicted probability that a project will be more
technically challenging than the hypothetical project            55
4.36 Expected duration of ATP intramural project compared to
the similar hypothetical project                                 56
4.37 Expected technical papers from the ATP intramural project
compared to the similar hypothetical project                     57
4.38 Expected new measurement technology from the ATP
intramural project compared to the similar hypothetical
project                                                          57
4.39 Expected new standards from the ATP intramural project
compared to the similar hypothetical project                     58
4.40 Expected new databases from the ATP intramural project
compared to the similar hypothetical project                     58
4.41 Probability of undertaking a broadly related research project
absent ATP intramural funding                                    59
4.42 Scope of ATP intramural project compared to the
hypothetical broadly defined project                             60
4.43 Technical challenge of ATP intramural project compared
to the broadly defined hypothetical project                      60
4.44 Expected duration of ATP intramural project compared to
the broadly defined hypothetical project                         60
4.45 Expected technical papers from the ATP intramural project
compared to the broadly defined hypothetical project             61
4.46 Expected new measurement technology from the ATP
intramural project compared to the broadly defined
hypothetical project                                             61
4.47 Expected new standards from the ATP intramural project
compared to the broadly defined hypothetical project             61
4.48 Expected new databases from the ATP intramural project
compared to the broadly defined hypothetical project             62
5.1 Initial candidate intramural research projects for
case study                                                       64
5.2 Sub-sample of nine candidate intramural research projects
for case study                                                   65
6.1 Industry benefits truncated at 10 years                      76
6.2 Estimated costs associated with SRM 2517a                    77

6.3 Estimated total costs and estimated total industry benefits associated with SRM 2517a — 78

6.4 Evaluation metrics for the SRM 2517a case study — 78

6.5 Revised evaluation metrics for the SRM 2517a case study using total benefits — 79

7.1 Estimated total costs and estimated total social benefits associated with injectable composite bone grafts — 86

7.2 Evaluation metrics for the injectable composite bone graft case study — 86

8.1 Estimated total costs and estimated total social benefits associated with ICM — 93

8.2 Evaluation metrics for the Internet commerce for manufacturing case study — 94

9.1 Estimated total costs and social benefits associated with the developed test method — 100

9.2 Evaluation metrics for the dielectrics case study — 101

# Acknowledgments

This book has benefited from the advice and assistance of many individuals. Special thanks go to Jeanne Powell of the US Advanced Technology Program within the National Institute of Standards and Technology (NIST). Were it not for her confidence in our research abilities, the study described herein would not have occurred. Along the way, she provided thoughtful comments and suggestions about the study and our presentation of our findings. Also, Sarah Gilbert, Barbara Goldstein, Jan Obrzut, Thomas Rhodes, and Francis Wang, all at NIST, provided invaluable technical guidance on the case studies. We also thank William Maloney of the World Bank, who offered many helpful thoughts and comments on the material in Chapter 2, Gary Anderson of NIST, who provided important suggestions for the material in Chapter 4, and Stephanie Shipp of NIST, who read the entire manuscript and offered many helpful suggestions. Of course, we are responsible for any remaining errors.

Also, we express our appreciation to Robert Langham and Terry Clague, both at Routledge, who enthusiastically supported this project from its inception.

Last, but most importantly, we thank our wives, Carol and Nancy, for providing the warmth and emotional sustenance that made this book, and its foundation research, possible.

# 1 Introduction

The US Advanced Technology Program (ATP) was established within the National Institute of Standards and Technology (NIST) through the Omnibus Trade and Competitiveness Act of 1988, and modified by the American Technology Preeminence Act of 1991. The goals of the ATP, as stated in its enabling legislation, are to assist US businesses in creating and applying the generic technology and results necessary to "[c]ommercialize significant new scientific discoveries and technologies rapidly, and refine manufacturing technologies."[1] More specifically:[2]

> The goal of the ATP is to benefit the U.S. economy by cost-sharing research with industry to foster new, innovative technologies. The ATP invests in risky, challenging technologies that have the potential for a big pay-off for the nation's economy. These technologies create opportunities for new, world-class products, services and industrial processes, benefiting not just the ATP participants, but other companies and industries and ultimately consumers and taxpayers as well. By reducing the early-stage R&D risks for individual companies, the ATP enables industry to pursue promising technologies which otherwise would be ignored or developed too slowly to compete in rapidly changing world markets.

ATP received its first appropriation from Congress in fiscal year (FY) 1990, and held its first general competition in that same year. Since then, ATP has announced 665 awards to single companies and joint ventures that involved more than 1,350 project participants. ATP awarded approximately $2.0 billion and industry has provided approximately $1.9 billion in matching funds.

ATP's intramural program refers to research and development (R&D) projects performed by NIST scientists in the Measurement and Standards Laboratories (MSLs) and paid for with ATP appropriations. ATP's statute permits the program to allocate up to 10 percent of its annual appropriation internally for standards development and technical activities in support of ATP's mission.

The Economic Assessment Office (EAO) of the ATP seeks to measure the economic impact of ATP's funding of high-risk, enabling technologies and also to increase understanding of economic relationships underlying technological change and economic growth. To this end, the EAO compiles data, conducts economic studies, and commissions studies by outside research organizations and economists.

In March 2000, the EAO was requested to perform an evaluation of ATP's intramural program following a performance audit of ATP's management of its intramural research projects conducted by the Office of Inspector General (OIG), US Department of Commerce. Findings of the OIG audit suggested that improvements were needed in some areas, and NIST was committed to a formal evaluation of intramural projects and to establishing routine procedures for collecting information to evaluate and track accomplishments on an ongoing basis. In particular, the OIG report stated:

*Recommendation*
We recommend that the Director of NIST...develop and implement policies and procedures that (1) require ATP managers to evaluate performance and (2) link the intramural funding results to ATP's performance measures and goals.

Intramural research awards were first made by ATP in FY 1992; however, formal policies and procedures for intramural funds allocations were not finalized until December 1993. Since 1997, ATP required that these intramural projects:

- emphasize generic basic research;
- relate to groups of ATP extramural projects (ATP's awards to industry for advanced technology development in furtherance of its fundamental mission);
- focus on measurement and standards that would facilitate the deployment and diffusion of ATP-funded technologies developed in ATP's extramural projects.

In 2001, the EAO asked us to conduct a systematic evaluation of ATP's intramural research program over the period 1992 through 2000 when nearly $99 million was allocated to researchers within NIST's MSLs. While the timing of our charge was motivated by the OIG's recommendation, the study we were commissioned to do represented an important part of ATP's long-standing and ongoing internal evaluation efforts.

Our efforts for ATP resulted in a comprehensive evaluation report, "Evaluation of ATP's Intramural Research Awards Program" (2004); this book is based, in part, on that report. To our knowledge, our efforts herein represent the first systematic study of a public agency's intramural research efforts. As such, it may be a template for others to follow.[3]

## ATP's intramural research program

The ATP intramural research program provides funding to NIST laboratories to conduct research to advance the US technology infrastructure in order to assist industry in continually improving products and services. Under the statute governing ATP, as previously mentioned, up to 10 percent of ATP's budget could be allocated for this research. As described below, the intramural program has stayed true to its mission but has changed in subtle ways.

ATP first made intramural research awards in FY 1992; however, formal policies and procedures for intramural funds allocations were not finalized until December 1993. From 1993 through 1996, ATP's Executive Officer calculated a tentative amount to be allocated to each ATP technical office, and the directors of each technical office were responsible for allocating funds among the program managers within that office.

During FY 1997, ATP's approach to intramural funding was revamped. Since 1997, the intramural funding has emphasized generic projects that cut across a group of ATP projects in order to provide the measurement and standards that facilitate the deployment and diffusion of ATP-developed technologies.

In 1998, ATP completed this transition. The emphasis of intramural research was broadened to take advantage of NIST's laboratory strengths and to build the research capabilities of the laboratories.

During the FYs 1992 through 2000, nearly $99 million was allocated toward intramural projects in the MSLs; see Figure 1.1. Funding ranged from $4.7 million in FY 1992 to almost $14 million in FY 2000. Only in 1992, 1993, and 2000 did the allocation for intramural funding come close to the allowable 10 percent allocation. The allocation for the remaining years ranged from a low of 3 percent in 1995 to 7 percent in 1998; see Table 1.1.

## Laboratory structure at NIST

The MSLs at NIST provide technical leadership for vital components of the nation's technology infrastructure needed by US industry to continually improve its products and services. Currently, there are seven

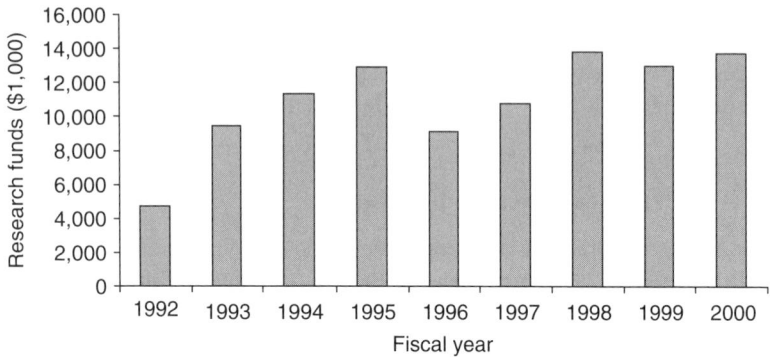

*Figure 1.1*  Allocation of intramural research funds, by FY.

*Table 1.1*  Intramural research funding as percentage of ATP allocations

| Fiscal year | Percentage |
| --- | --- |
| 1992 | 9.5 |
| 1993 | 9.9 |
| 1994 | 5.7 |
| 1995 | 3.0 |
| 1996 | 4.1 |
| 1997 | 4.8 |
| 1998 | 7.2 |
| 1999 | 6.4 |
| 2000 | 9.7 |

Notes
The FY 1993 percentage does not include carry over funding from FY 1992. See notes to Table 1.2.

research laboratories at NIST:[4]

1    The Electronics and Electrical Engineering Laboratory (EEEL) promotes US economic growth by providing measurement capability of high impact focused primarily on the critical needs of the US electronics and electrical industries, and their customers and suppliers.
2    The Manufacturing Engineering Laboratory (MEL) performs research and development of measurements, standards, and infrastructure technology as related to manufacturing.

3 The Chemical Science and Technology Laboratory (CSTL) provides chemical measurement infrastructure to enhance US industry's productivity and competitiveness; assure equity in trade; and improve public health, safety, and environmental quality.

4 The Physics Laboratory (PL) supports US industry by providing measurement services and research for electronic, optical, and radiation technologies.

5 The Materials Science and Engineering Laboratory (MSEL) stimulates the more effective production and use of materials by working with materials suppliers and users to assure the development and implementation of the measurement and standards infrastructure for materials.

6 The Building and Fire Research Laboratory (BFRL) enhances the competitiveness of US industry and public safety by developing performance prediction methods, measurement technologies, and technical advances needed to assure the life cycle quality and economy of constructed facilities.

7 The Information Technology Laboratory (ITL) works with industry, research, and government organizations to develop and demonstrate tests, test methods, reference data, proof of concept implementations, and other infrastructural technologies.[5]

Figure 1.2 shows the inter-laboratory distribution of intramural funds over the 1992–2000 time period. The MSEL, received the largest share (almost one-fourth of the funding) from 1992 to 2000. Three other laboratories, EEEL, MEL, and CSTL, each received about one-sixth of the funding over

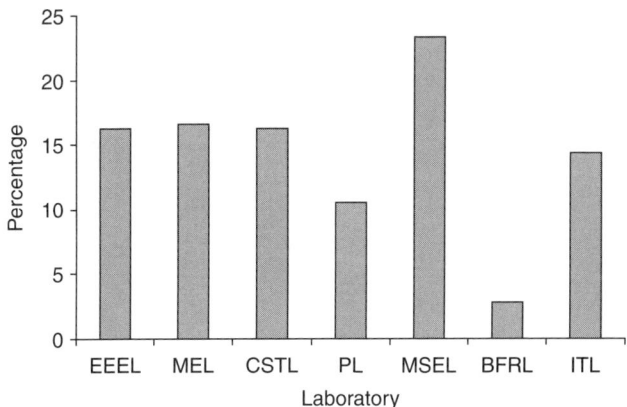

*Figure 1.2* Allocation of intramural research funds, by laboratory.

Table 1.2 Allocation of intramural research funds, by laboratory and by year (in percentages)

| Measurement and standards laboratory | FY 1992 | FY 1993 | FY 1994 | FY 1995 | FY 1996 | FY 1997 | FY 1998 | FY 1999 | FY 2000 |
|---|---|---|---|---|---|---|---|---|---|
| Electronics and Electrical Engineering (81) | 20 | 24 | 26 | 17 | 12 | 11 | 14 | 15 | 11 |
| Manufacturing Engineering (82) | 23 | 19 | 17 | 17 | 18 | 17 | 17 | 14 | 13 |
| Chemical Science and Technology (83) | 10 | 12 | 15 | 9 | 12 | 18 | 20 | 21 | 22 |
| Physics (84) | 9 | 11 | 11 | 8 | 7 | 7 | 12 | 14 | 13 |
| Material Science and Engineering (85) | 17 | 15 | 21 | 26 | 38 | 29 | 22 | 20 | 21 |
| Building and Fire Research (86) | 1 | 3 | 3 | 0.4 | 4 | 3 | 3 | 4 | 4 |
| Information Technology (89) | 19 | 16 | 6 | 23 | 9 | 16 | 13 | 12 | 17 |
| Total ($1,000s rounded) | 4,700 | 9,476 | 11,373 | 12,956 | 9,104 | 10,737 | 13,804 | 13,037 | 13,796 |

Source: ATP. ATP's FY is October through September.

Notes
Laboratory classification numbers are in parentheses.

On February 16, 1997, NIST abolished the Computer Systems Laboratory (87) and the Computing and Applied Mathematics Laboratory (88) and combined the two to form the ITL (89). Intramural allocations in FY 1992 through 1996 to the former laboratories are shown in the table as allocations to the ITL for purposes of comparisons. However, in the statistical analysis of the NIST scientist survey results, these laboratories are separated.

When intramural funds were allocated to a project involving scientists from more than one MSL, all funds were allocated to the MSL of the first-named scientist.

FY 1993 allocations include $2,754,000 of carry over FY 1992 funding.

*Table 1.3* Allocation of intramural research funds, by laboratory (in percentages), 1992–2000

| Measurement and standards laboratory | Aggregated over all years |
|---|---|
| Electronics and Electrical Engineering (81) | 16 |
| Manufacturing Engineering (82) | 17 |
| Chemical Science and Technology (83) | 16 |
| Physics (84) | 11 |
| Material Science and Engineering (85) | 24 |
| Building and Fire Research (86) | 3 |
| Information Technology (89) | 14 |
| Total ($1,000s rounded) | 98,983 |

the 9-year period, and ITL received almost the same amount. The PL and BFRL received the remaining funds.

Table 1.2 shows both the total ATP funds allocated to intramural research as well as the distribution of those funds across each MSL, by FY. Between 1992 and 2000, the relative distributions across MSLs show declines in the proportion of intramural funds going to the EEEL and MEL balanced by increases in the CSTL, PL, MSEL, and BFRL. The dollar allocations in the last row of the table vary by year (see also Figure 1.1), but so has the overall ATP budget.

Table 1.3 shows the aggregated percentage allocations across MSLs in percentage terms. They provide the actual numerical values for the percentages conveyed visually in Figure 1.2.

The FY data in Table 1.2 and the aggregate data in Table 1.3 also show how intramural research funds have been allocated across MSLs in the context of the evolution of criteria for the selection of intramural research projects. In FYs 1994 through 1998, ATP funding was applied to specific focused program areas – multi-year efforts aimed to achieve specific, well-defined technology and business goals. Beginning in FY 1999, all competition returned to being open to all areas of technology, a feature that has long been the hallmark of general competitions.

## Evaluation framework for the study

Our general framework for evaluating ATP's intramural research awards program builds on the framework in which ATP evaluates itself, namely:

inputs → outputs → outcomes → impacts.[6]

Within the context of the overall ATP program, inputs include funding and research partnership formation; outputs include knowledge, in general, and inventions, in particular; outcomes include acceleration of research and commercial applications of research results; and impacts include societal benefits.

In the case of the intramural awards program, which supports internal projects that apply the research capabilities of NIST's laboratories to support ATP's mission, this general evaluation framework remains applicable.

The intramural research awards program enhances the activities of the NIST laboratories. In an ideal experiment, one would compare the outputs and outcomes associated with research within NIST laboratories *with* ATP intramural funding to the outputs and outcomes associated with comparable NIST laboratory research *without* ATP intramural funding. Another option would measure the outputs and outcomes associated with research in NIST laboratories over time and compare them between periods when ATP intramural funding was available and when it was not, all other things remaining constant. Neither evaluation approach is possible because comparable research projects could not be identified and because the relative newness of the intramural program made the time frame for a time series study too short to accommodate research projects starting and being completed.

Thus, the best available approach encompassed several parts. NIST scientists who received ATP funding were asked to complete a survey that asked them to compare the outputs and outcomes from their research with hypothetically similar projects and broad NIST laboratory benchmarks. In addition, the output from the ATP funded project was compared with the same type of output for all of the NIST laboratories' projects. Finally, because impacts (such as industrial impacts per the mission statement of the NIST laboratories) could not be documented from such a survey, detailed case studies of projects that received ATP intramural support were conducted. Such case studies are not intended to be representative of all funded projects, but rather to illustrate the breadth of societal benefits associated with ATP intramural funding.

## Outline of the book

The following chapter sets forth an economic rationale for public research institutions such as NIST – a federal laboratory, and ATP is within NIST's administrative structure. Then, two chapters summarize the findings from the first part of the intramural program evaluation – a survey of all ATP intramural project principal investigators (PIs). The survey design and methodology is discussed in Chapter 3 and the quantitative results from the survey are summarized and discussed in Chapter 4.

The next five chapters discuss the methodology for and results from selected case studies of ATP-funded intramural research projects performed in the NIST labs. In Chapter 5 the methodology for selection of those studies is summarized, as are the metrics relevant for characterizing the spillover impacts of the knowledge base developed in these projects to industry and society. Chapters 6 through 9 are the case studies.

Chapter 10 concludes the book with general observations about alternative templates for public-sector program evaluation.

# 2 The role of public research institutions[1]

## Government's role in innovation

The theoretical basis for government's role in market activity is based on the concept of market failure. Market failure is typically attributed to market power, imperfect information, externalities, and public goods. The explicit application of market failure to justify government's role in innovation – in R&D activity in particular – is a relatively recent phenomenon within public policy.

Many point in the United States to President George Bush's 1990 *US Technology Policy* as that nation's first formal domestic technology policy statement. Albeit an important initial policy effort, it however failed to articulate a foundation for government's role in innovation and technology. Rather, it implicitly assumed that government had a role, and then set forth the general statement (EOP, 1990, p. 2):

> The goal of U.S. technology policy is to make the best use of technology in achieving the national goals of improved quality of life for all Americans, continued economic growth, and national security.

President William Clinton took a major step forward from the 1990 policy statement in his 1994 *Economic Report of the President* by articulating first principles about why government should be involved in the technological process (CEA, 1994, p. 191):

> The goal of technology policy is not to substitute the government's judgment for that of private industry in deciding which potential "winners" to back. Rather, the point is to correct market failure…[2]

Subsequent Executive Office policy statements have echoed this theme; *Science in the National Interest* (OSTP, 1994) and *Science and*

*Technology: Shaping the Twenty-First Century* (OSTP, 1998) are among the examples. President Clinton's 2000 *Economic Report of the President* (CEA, 2000, p. 99) elaborated upon the concept of market failure as part of US technology policy:

> Rather than support technologies that have clear and immediate commercial potential (which would likely be developed by the private sector without government support), government should seek out new technologies that will create benefits with large spillovers to society at large.

Relatedly, Martin and Scott (2000, p. 438) observe:

> Limited appropriability, financial market failure, external benefits to the production of knowledge, and other factors suggest that strict reliance on a market system will result in underinvestment in innovation, relative to the socially desirable level. This creates a *prima facie* case in favor of public intervention to promote innovative activity.

## Underinvestment in R&D

Market failure, as we address it in this chapter and of the type which could specifically be termed "technological or innovation market failure," refers to a condition under which the market, including both the R&D-investing producers of a technology and the users of the technology, underinvests, from society's standpoint, in a particular technology. Such underinvestment occurs because conditions exist that prevent organizations from fully realizing or appropriating the benefits created by their investments.

The following explanation of market failure and the reasons for market failure follow closely Arrow's (1962) seminal work in which he identified three sources of market failure related to knowledge-based innovative activity – "indivisibilities, inappropriability, and uncertainty" (p. 609).[3]

To explain, consider a marketable technology to be produced through an R&D process where conditions prevent full appropriation of the benefits from technological advancement by the R&D-investing firm. Other firms in the market or in related markets will realize some of the profits from the innovation, and of course consumers will typically place a higher value on a product than the price paid for it. The R&D-investing firm will then calculate, because of such conditions, that the marginal benefits it can receive from a unit investment in such R&D will be less than could be earned in the absence of the conditions reducing the appropriated benefits of R&D below their potential, namely the full social benefits. Thus, the R&D-investing firm may

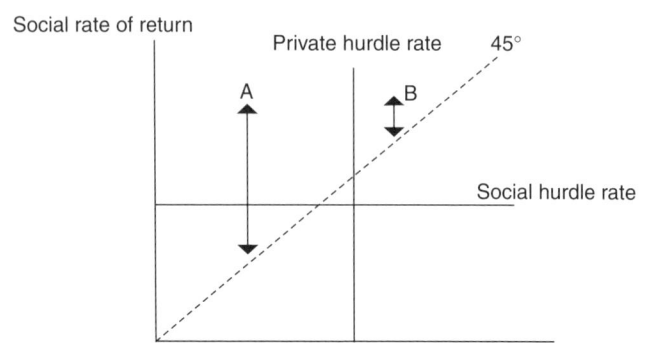

*Figure 2.1* Spillover gap between social and private rates of return to R&D.

underinvest in R&D, relative to what it would have chosen as its investment in the absence of the conditions. Stated alternatively, the R&D-investing firm may determine that its private rate of return is less than its private hurdle rate and therefore it will not undertake socially valuable R&D.

The basic concept can be illustrated with Figure 2.1, which follows from Tassey (1997) and Jaffe (1998). The social rate of return is measured on the vertical axis along with society's hurdle rate on investments in R&D. The private rate of return is measured on the horizontal axis along with the private hurdle rate on R&D. A 45° line (dashed) is imposed on the figure under the assumption that the social rate of return from an R&D investment will at least equal the private rate of return from the same investment. Two separate R&D projects are labeled as projects A and B. Each is shown, for illustrative purposes only, with the same social rate of return.

For project A, the private rate of return is less than the private hurdle rate because of barriers to innovation and technology. As such, the private firm will not choose to invest in project A, although the social benefits from undertaking project A would be substantial.

The principle of market failure illustrated in the figure relates to appropriability of returns to investment. The vertical distance shown with the double arrow for project A is called the spillover gap; it results from the additional value society would receive above what the private firm would receive if project A were undertaken. What the firm would receive (along the 45° line) is less than its hurdle rate because the firm is unable to appropriate all of the returns that spillover to society. Project A is the type of project in which public resources should be invested to ensure that the project is undertaken.

In comparison, project B yields the same social rate of return as project A, but most of that return can be appropriated by the innovator, and the private rate of return is greater than the private hurdle rate. Hence, project B is one for which the private sector has an incentive to invest on its own or, alternatively stated, there is no economic justification for public resources being allocated to support project B.

For projects of type A where significant spillovers occur, government's role has typically been to provide funding or technology infrastructure through public research institutions that lowers the marginal cost of investment so that the marginal private rate of return exceeds the private hurdle rate.

Note that the private hurdle rate is greater than the social hurdle rate in the figure. This is primarily because of management's (and employees') risk aversion and issues related to the availability and cost of capital. These factors represent an additional source of market failure that is related to uncertainty. For example, because most private firms are risk averse (i.e. the penalty from lower than expected returns is weighted more heavily than the benefits from greater than expected returns), they require a higher hurdle rate of return compared to society as a whole that is closer to being risk neutral.[4]

To reduce market failures associated with inappropriability and uncertainty, government typically engages in activities to reduce technical and market risk (actual and perceived). These activities include, but are not limited to, the activities of public research institutions, as discussed below. The following section discusses several circumstances – termed "barriers to technology" – that cause market failure and an underinvestment in R&D.

### Barriers to innovation and technology

There are a number of factors that can explain why a firm will perceive that its expected private rate of return will fall below its hurdle rate.[5] Individuals will differ not only about a listing of such factors because they are not generally mutually exclusive, but also they will differ about the relative importance of one factor compared to another in whatever taxonomy is chosen.

First, high technical risk (i.e. outcomes may not be technically sufficient to meet needs) may cause market failure given that when the firm is successful, the private returns fall short of the social returns. The risk of the activity being undertaken is greater than the firm can accept, although if successful there would be very large benefits to society as a whole. Society would like the investment to be made, but from the perspective of the firm, the present value of expected returns is less than the investment cost and is thus less than the amount yielding its acceptable return on investment.

Second, high technical risk can relate to high commercial or market risk (although technically sufficient, the market may not accept the innovation – reasons can include factors listed subsequently such as imitation or competing substitutes or interoperability issues) as well as to technical risk when the requisite R&D is highly capital intensive. The project may require too much capital for any one firm to feel comfortable with the outlay. The minimum cost of conducting research is thus viewed as excessive relative to the firm's overall R&D budget, which considers the costs of outside financing and the risks of bankruptcy. In this case, the firm will not make the investment, although society would be better off if it had, because the project does not appear to be profitable from the firm's private perspective.

Third, many R&D projects are characterized by a lengthy time interval until a commercial product reaches the market. The time expected to complete the R&D and the time until commercialization of the R&D results are long, and the realization of a cash flow from the R&D investment is in the distant future. If a private firm faces greater risk than society does, and as a result requires a greater rate of return and hence applies a higher discount rate than society does, it will value future returns less than does society. Because the private discount rate exceeds the social discount rate, there may be underinvestment, and the underinvestment increases as the time to market increases because the difference in the rate is compounded and has a bigger effect on returns further into the future.

Fourth, it is not uncommon for the scope of potential markets to be broader than the scope of the individual firm's market strategies so the firm will not perceive or project economic benefits from all potential market applications of the technology. As such, the firm will consider in its investment decisions only those returns that it can appropriate within the boundaries of its market strategies. While the firm may recognize that there are spillover benefits to other markets, and while it could possibly appropriate them, such benefits are ignored or discounted heavily relative to the discount weight that would apply to society. A similar situation arises when the requirements for conducting R&D demand multidisciplinary research teams; unique research facilities not generally available with individual companies; or "fusing" technologies from heretofore separate, non-interacting parties. The possibility for opportunistic behavior in such thin markets may make it impossible, at a reasonable cost, for a single firm to share capital assets even if there were not R&D information sharing difficulties to compound the problem. If society, perhaps through a technology-based public institution, could act as an honest broker to coordinate a cooperative multi-firm effort, then the social costs of the multidisciplinary research might be less than the market costs.[6]

Fifth, the evolving nature of markets requires investments in combinations of technologies that, if they existed, would reside in different industries that are not integrated. Because such conditions often transcend the R&D strategy of firms, such investments are not likely to be pursued. That is not only because of the lack of recognition of possible benefit areas or the perceived inability to appropriate whatever results, but also because coordinating multiple players in a timely and efficient manner is cumbersome and costly. Again, as with the multidisciplinary research teams, society may be able to use a technology-based public institution to act as an honest broker and reduce costs below those that the market would face.

Sixth, a situation can exist when the nature of the technology is such that it is difficult to assign intellectual property rights. Knowledge and ideas developed by a firm that invests in technology may spillover to other firms during the R&D phase or after the new technology is introduced into the market. If the information creates value for the firms that benefit from the spillovers, then other things being equal, the innovating firms may underinvest in the technology. Relatedly, when competition in the development of new technology is very intense, each firm, knowing that the probability of being the successful innovator is low, may not anticipate sufficient returns to cover costs. Further, even if the firm innovates, intense competition at the application stage can result because of competing substitute goods, whether patented or not. Especially when the cost of imitation is low, an individual firm will anticipate such competition and may therefore not anticipate returns sufficient to cover its R&D investment costs. Of course, difficulties appropriating returns need not always inhibit R&D investment (Baldwin and Scott, 1987). First-mover advantages associated with customer acceptance and demand, as well as increasing returns as markets are penetrated and production expanded, can imply that an innovator wins most (or at least a sufficient portion to support the investment) of the rewards even if it does not "take all."

Seventh, industry structure may raise the cost of market entry for applications of the technology. The broader market environment in which a new technology will be sold can significantly reduce incentives to invest in its development and commercialization because of what some scholars have called technological lock-in and path dependency.[7] Many technology-based products are part of larger systems of products. Under such industry structures, if a firm is contemplating investing in the development of a new product but perceives a risk that the product, even if technically successful, will not interface with other products in the system, the additional cost of attaining compatibility or interoperability may reduce the expected rate of return to the point that the project is not undertaken. Similarly, multiple sub-markets may evolve, each with its own interface requirements, thereby preventing economies of scale or network externalities from being realized. Again, society, perhaps through a technology-based public institution, may be able to help the market's participants coordinate successful compatibility and interoperability.

Eighth, situations exist where the complexity of a technology makes agreement with respect to product performance between buyer and seller costly. Sharing of the information needed for the exchange and development of technology can render the needed transactions between independent firms in the market prohibitively costly if the incentives for opportunistic behavior are to be reduced to a reasonable level with what Teece (1980) calls obligational contracts. Teece emphasizes that the successful transfer of technology from one firm to another often requires careful teamwork with purposeful interactions between the seller and the buyer of the technology. In such circumstances, both the seller of the technology and the buyer of the technology are exposed to hazards of opportunism. Sellers, for example, may fear that buyers will capture the know-how too cheaply or use it in unexpected ways. Buyers may worry that the sellers will fail to provide the necessary support to make the technology work in the new environment; or they may worry that after learning about the buyer's operations in sufficient detail to transfer the technology successfully, the seller would back away from the transfer and instead enter the buyer's industry as a technologically sophisticated competitor. Once again, if society can use a technology-based public institution to act as an honest broker, the social costs of sharing technology may be less than market costs.

These eight factors that create, individually or in combination, barriers to innovation and technology and thus lead to a private underinvestment in R&D are listed in Table 2.1. While we have discussed these factors individually above, and have listed them in Table 2.1 as if they are discrete phenomena, they are interrelated and overlapping, although in principle any one factor could be sufficient to cause a private firm to underinvest in R&D.

*Table 2.1* Factors creating barriers to innovation and technology

| | |
|---|---|
| 1 | High technical risk associated with the underlying R&D |
| 2 | High capital costs to undertake the underlying R&D |
| 3 | Long time to complete the R&D and commercialize the resulting technology |
| 4 | Underlying R&D spills over to multiple markets and is not appropriable |
| 5 | Market success of the technology depends on technologies in different industries |
| 6 | Property rights cannot be assigned to the underlying R&D |
| 7 | Resulting technology must be compatible and interoperable with other technologies |
| 8 | High risk of opportunistic behavior when sharing information about the technology |

## The role of public research institutions

Public research institutions – their intramural research as well as their focused extramural research activity – could overcome many of the barriers to innovation and technology discussed in the previous section.

For the purpose of describing the rationale for public research institutions that provide, intramurally or extramurally, infrastructure technology needed by industry, we use a definition of risk that is focused on the operational concern with the downside outcomes for an investment. The shortfalls of the private expected outcomes from society's expected returns reflect appropriability problems. There are several related technological and market factors that will cause private firms to appropriate less return and to face greater risk than society does. These factors underlie what Arrow (1962) identified as the non-exclusivity and public good characteristics of investments in the creation of knowledge. The private firms' incomplete appropriation of social returns in the context of technical and market risk can make risk in its operational sense unacceptably large for the private firm considering an investment.

Operationally and with reference to Figure 2.1, Tassey (1992, 1997, 2005), for example, defines risk as the probability that a project's rate of return falls below a required, private rate of return or private hurdle rate (as opposed to simply deviating from an expected return).[8] As illustrated in Link and Scott (2001a) – both in concept and in terms of the specific projects performed by the private sector with subsidies and oversight from the Advanced Technology Program within the US NIST – for many socially desirable investments, the private firm faces an unacceptably large probability of a rate of return that falls short of its private hurdle rate. Yet, from society's perspective, the probability of a rate of return that is less than the social hurdle rate is sufficiently small that the project is still worthwhile.

Martin and Scott (2000, pp. 438–439) make the point that the design of appropriate public policy should match the policy with the specific source of underinvestment. In that light, they identify several roles for public research institutions. Given the types of research they perform, such institutions could be called standards and infrastructure technology institutions, and we focus in this chapter on their role within a national innovation system. Specific activities of those institutions are matched with specific sources of underinvestment in research, and the various activities are illustrated with examples from case studies.

One role for a public research institution is to facilitate the promulgation and adoption of standards and thereby, for example, reduce the risk associated with standards for new technology as inputs are developed for using industries such as in the sectors developing software, equipment, and instruments. We are using the term "standards" in a general sense to refer to voluntary performance protocols and interoperability standards, test methods, and standard reference materials. Although one can find examples where observers have thought that product standards were used in anti-competitive ways, the role for public research institutions is quite general and important, encompassing several types of standards. The public institution with research capability can respond to industry's needs for standards, working with industry to develop them while serving as an honest broker providing impartial mediation of disputes that could not be provided by a private firm with a proprietary interest in the outcomes.[9] In the absence of the public research institution, industry would have incurred higher costs to replace the public standards activities than the actual costs to the public institution for those activities. Further, the quality of the more costly private standards activities would have been less than the quality of the public standards activities.

For another role, public research institutions can oversee extension services to facilitate technology transfer in sectors such as light industry or agriculture when, for example, small firms, facing limited appropriability from their investments in new technologies yet providing large external benefits to the economy as a whole, apply inputs developed in supplying industries. Such extension services can make possible a vibrant entrepreneurial sector of smaller firms that stimulates the adoption and diffusion of new technology and also innovation, technological advance, and economic growth.

The positive impact of such an entrepreneurial sector has been documented by many scholars – for example, Audretsch (1995) – and in the last two decades recognition of its importance for economic growth has increased and become widespread. Imperfections in credit markets, opportunistic behavior by larger firms that might provide resources to small entrepreneurial businesses, and the unappropriated external benefits from entrepreneurial businesses might require public support of extension services to avoid underinvestment in the transfer technologies. Although the argument for public research institutions with research capability is not as strong as it is in the foregoing role with standards, public research institutions such as the US NIST are in a good position to foster the technology transfer provided by extension programs. Such public institutions have knowledge of the key technologies, have working relationships with the industries supplying the technologies, and can assist with the transfer the technologies without opportunistic exploitation of the small firms, allowing them to grow as independent sources of initiative and growth.[10]

For a third role, a public research institute can serve as the coordinator and facilitator for cooperative R&D efforts joining industry, universities, and government in research that is subsidized by the government. The several projects studied by Hall *et al.* (2003) provide examples of such cooperative R&D efforts. Such cooperative research with a public research institution as the facilitator is often necessary to coordinate the development of infrastructure technologies as well as pre-competitive generic technologies that are at the heart of the development of complex systems involving high cost, risk, and limited appropriability. These complex systems are developed, for example, in aerospace, electrical and electronics technology, and tele-communications and computer technologies. While the coordination of cooperative efforts that transcend the solely market-based activities of industry is arguably an important and central role for government, the key question is whether a public research institution playing that coordinating role actually needs to have a research capacity itself. Based on the case studies in our other writings, we believe that in many cases the answer is "Yes." For example, the ATP relies on the research capability of NIST to ensure not only sound oversight of the competitions for the government's chosen research projects that will be performed by industry with partial public funding, but to provide as well coordinated research developing infrastructure technologies that support the advances in technology that the ATP hopes to foster through its awards for publicly subsidized and privately performed research.[11]

Finally, for industrial applications of technologies with high science content, where the knowledge base originates outside of the commercial sector, the creators of the knowledge may not recognize the potential applications or effectively communicate the new developments to potential users. As a fourth role in a national innovation system, a public research institution can facilitate the diffusion of advances from research in these cases – such as in biotechnology, chemistry, materials science, and pharmaceuticals – where the applications have high science content. This fourth role is one of facilitating communication and dissemination of ideas from science that can then be used by many sectors to advance applied research and development. In many cases, government funds will have been used by universities to develop the basic science, because the ideas have a strong public good component and there would not have been sufficient incentive to develop them without government funding. Once the basic science is available, the knowledgeable public research institution with expertise in both research and connections to industry can help to disseminate the information widely.

Granted that basic research with economy-wide implications and very long time horizons is unlikely to be undertaken by private firms, are there reasons – incentive problems and market failures – that would require that the basic research should be *performed* by the government and not by, for example, the government's financing of private universities? That is, are there reasons that the fourth role for the public research institution would include not only working to communicate basic science, transferring it to industry in ways that focus on the industrial usefulness of the basic science, but the public laboratory would actually do basic science itself. Although, in our experience with the work done in the US government laboratories, we have observed some fairly basic research (such as in the materials science involved in the dielectrics case discussed in Chapter 9), even the most basic research is quite applied – for example, using the basic science created in universities to develop new measurement technology. Conceivably there are incentive issues that may dictate the performance of certain types of basic research in the laboratories of public research institutions. By their nature, the research objectives of the government may differ from the interests of universities and their researchers, and it is possible that some goals of the government's basic research agenda would not align well with the current academic interests. Stated differently, academic researchers might find it beneath them to do the science that the public happens to want at a particular time. Another possibility is that academic researchers cannot always take the long view (especially given that the long view can change as political administrations change) needed to develop a government-mandated strand of science, in the detail needed, simply because of the constraints of turning out sufficient publications of sufficient variety and quality in the context of review and promotion for the researchers. Laboring in some public service vineyard for a decade or more may not have the necessary academic rewards to ensure survival in the university system. A public laboratory scientist is freed from such constraints and the public laboratory can set its own reward structure that is sensitive to the fact that political administrations change and the scientific imperatives of government can change. Finally, national security may dictate that some types of research are performed in government laboratories with heightened security rather than in the more open environment of university laboratories.

In all of the foregoing roles for the public research institution, the institution is not only an honest broker providing technological services – standards, standard reference materials, calibrations traceable to the standards, technology transfer and diffusion of scientific advances – without a proprietary, rivalrous, market-based interest. As well, the public research institution's research capability is an integral part of developing and maintaining standards and other technological services. The institution is not just an administrator, but an organization with real scientific and engineering expertise. In matters of generic and infrastructure technology, the institution is an honest broker with leading-edge research capabilities and close working relationships with industry allowing it to understand industry's needs and continually develop and maintain the standards and services that industry relies on for its productivity.

The theoretical foundation for public sector involvement in any aspect of the innovation process logically leads to a discussion of public accountability, meaning that the public sector is also responsible for evaluating the social benefits of its actions.

# 3 Survey design and methodology

In the fall of 2001, with input from the ATP, we designed a survey instrument for all ATP intramural project PIs. The instrument was pre-tested and sent electronically to the 278 project PIs at NIST at the time. It is reproduced as Table 3.1.

*Table 3.1* Survey instrument for NIST PIs

*Project title:*

*Years and funding:*

Q1  Did the scope of this intramural research project complement an ongoing research agenda in your laboratory, or did it help to initiate a new research direction – that is, did it expand NIST's competencies in new areas? Please explain.

Q2  Please provide complete bibliographic citations for all technical papers that resulted from this project and were published in professional journals, conference proceedings, or elsewhere.

Q3  Please provide complete citations for all patents filed or received that resulted from this project.

Q4  Approximately, how many professional presentations (outside of NIST) related to this project have been given? _____
And, to what types of groups?

Q5  Apart from publications, patents, and presentations, please list any other "technical outputs" that resulted from this project such as new measurement technology(ies), new standards, or new verified databases.

Q6  Did this project contribute to the basis for subsequent NIST competency awards, other sources of federal funding to the laboratory, or CRADA activity? If so, please provide details.

Q7  Briefly, please offer your perception of the benefits that industry (please specify the industry(ies)) has received or will receive in the future from the results of this project.

*Table 3.1* Continued

*Project title:*
*Years and funding:*

Q8  If you have the names and phone numbers of individuals in industry with whom we may talk to learn more about the benefits that their industry has received or will receive in the future from the results of this project, please provide that information.

Q9  To conclude this survey, we would like to ask you to address these hypothetical questions. When making comparisons, please consider a hypothetical project with an amount of funding comparable to your ATP intramural project. If you had not received funding for this ATP intramural research project, would you have undertaken a project with *similar* goals and milestones?
    Yes _____ (please go to Q10)
    No _____ (please go to Q11)

Q10  As a result of ATP funding, are you *ahead/in the same place/behind* in achieving *similar* goals and milestones? _____
    If *ahead*, by approximately how many months? _____

    How does this ATP intramural project compare to the project with *similar* goals and milestones that you would have undertaken without ATP funding (and we ask this question in an effort to characterize differences between projects with and without ATP funding and not to value one category of project over another)?
    Is it broader in scope? *Yes/No* _____
    Is it more technically challenging? *Yes/No* _____
    Is the expected duration/time to completion *longer/the same/shorter*? _____
    Do you think that ATP funding led to *more/less/different* technical outputs (as listed below) compared to the technical outputs from the project you would have undertaken without ATP funding?
    Technical papers _____
    Patents _____
    New measurement technology _____
    New standards _____
    New databases _____
    Please describe any other differences.

Q11  Would you have undertaken a project in the same broadly-defined research area as your ATP intramural project? *Yes/No* _____

    If *Yes*, How does this ATP intramural project compare to that project (and we ask this question in an effort to characterize differences between projects with and without ATP funding and not to value one category of project over another)?
    Is it broader in scope? *Yes/No* _____
    Is it more technically challenging? *Yes/No* _____
    Is the expected duration/time to completion *longer/the same/shorter*? _____
    Do you think that ATP funding led to *more/less/different* technical outputs (as listed below) compared to the technical outputs from the project you would have undertaken without ATP funding?

(*Table 3.1 continued*)

*Table 3.1* Continued

| |
|---|
| *Project title:* |
| *Years and funding:* |

Technical papers _____
Patents _____
New measurement technology _____
New standards _____
New databases _____
Please describe any other differences.
Again, thank you for your timely participation in this important study.

The following statement prefaced the survey in the electronic communication with each PI.

Dear PI,
As you may know, the Office of Inspector General of the Department of Commerce has requested that the Economic Assessment Office of the Advanced Technology Program (ATP) conduct an economic evaluation of their intramural funding program.

John Scott (Dartmouth College) and I (University of North Carolina at Greensboro) have been asked by Jeanne Powell in the ATP office to undertake this project.

As part of our assignment, we have been instructed to survey all individuals who have received an ATP intramural research award. Attached to this email is a generic survey instrument (WORD document) approved by ATP.

As Linda Beth Schilling stated in her recent email to OU Directors about this survey: "Overall, we hope the results of this survey will help us know how to better collaborate with the laboratories using intramural funding. In addition, we expect statistics from this to be useful in summarizing some of the laboratories' achievements as a result of the funding – we would love to brag more about the results on our website to help with diffusing results to industry."

Would you please complete a separate survey instrument for each ATP intramural research project (just copy the instrument as many times as relevant). If there are co-researchers on an award, please respond from your perspective as PI. You may leave blank any questions that do not apply to your research. If your intramural research project was active in the early years of the program and you no longer have files on that project, feel free to return a blank instrument with a notation to that effect.

Our records show that you have received the following intramural research awards: [Name of award listed along with funding allocations by year]

Again, please fill out an instrument for *each* award. We would both appreciate receiving your completed forms within 2 weeks. In advance, thank you for your timely cooperation.

The following outputs resulting from the intramural funding are considered within this survey: the scope of laboratory research (Q1), publications (Q2), patents (Q3), presentations (Q4), and other technical outputs (Q5). Additionally, outcomes are considered: leveraging of R&D funding (Q6 and Q9), cycle time of R&D (Q10), and the technical nature of R&D (Q11).

The PI for an intramural project was identified to be that individual listed on the ATP intramural project budget allocation records at the time the award was made. If a project was awarded to more than one researcher, it was assumed that the first named researcher was the PI. During FY 1992 through FY 2000, ATP funded 1,052 intramural projects. The 278 surveyed PIs were associated with 510 of these projects.

An introductory letter from ATP's Deputy Director informed Operating Unit Directors that the results of this survey are intended to help ATP know how to collaborate better with the laboratories using intramural funding. In addition, ATP expects statistics from the survey to be useful in summarizing some of the laboratories' achievements as a result of the funding.

In early December 2001, each PI who did not respond to the first survey was sent a reminder email. No surveys were received after the end of 2001.

A total of 209 surveys were returned with at least some information for one or more projects. This represents a response by 43 percent of the 278 PIs; the surveys included at least some information for 41 percent of the 510 projects; 30 reported that no information was available on the project because of its age.

The survey contains several open-ended questions, but very few PIs responded to them. Thus, we do not present discussion of those sparse responses herein.

Response rates differed for each question. Generally, a PI was *less likely* to respond to a question for a particular project the greater the number of intramural research awards that the PI received, and the greater the age of the project. In contrast, response was *more likely* the larger the budget of the project.

These three response-determining factors appear intuitive. The more projects for which a PI was asked information, the greater the total time burden to the PI and the less likely he or she would respond. Similarly, greater time would be needed by the PI to retrieve requested information about an older project. PIs with larger budgets perhaps responded more often because of the breadth and scope of the research was greater; hence its importance to the PI's research agenda was greater. Statistical adjustments were made for non-response bias, as discussed in detail in Chapter 4.

# 4 Quantitative analysis of the effects of ATP intramural funding

## Overview of the findings

The survey information collected from NIST PIs relates to:

- project outputs and outcomes;
- comparisons with projects that would have been undertaken in the absence of ATP intramural funding.

Scope of project, publications, and presentations are an integral part of the research mission of NIST scientists and are used as measures of project outputs. Patents are not an integral part of NIST's intramural program mission, yet some early projects produced patents. The results, adjusted for response bias, from the NIST PI survey suggest the following:

- ATP funding potentially enhances NIST competencies by initiating a new research direction and thereby expanding the scope of the PI's laboratory research, or by complementing the PI's ongoing research agenda. On average, PIs perceive the scope of laboratory research was expanded in one of five projects.
- Less than one publication resulted from each intramural project (there were on average two publications for every three projects), and each publication was cited in the literature by someone who was not involved in the project about one and two-thirds times (there were on average about five citations for every three publications).[1]
- On average, one patent results from about every 20 projects among the reporting projects.
- On average, one presentation results from each project.
- Over 30 percent of the reporting ATP intramural projects leveraged other sources of funding such as NIST competency awards or Cooperative Research and Development Agreement (CRADA) activity.

The quantities of publications, patents, and so forth describe absolute measures of output performance, but do the numbers reflect good performance? That is, relative to NIST projects in general, do the ATP-funded NIST projects perform well? We were able to provide one actual comparison, and for multiple measures of performance we were able to collect and analyze the PIs' assessments of the performance differences between ATP intramural projects and hypothetical, similar projects in the NIST laboratories that would not have ATP support.

Comprehensive NIST benchmark data were available only for one output measure – publications per million dollars of budget. Actual publication performance for the reporting ATP-intramural projects outperformed publication performance from a typical NIST project as revealed in the benchmark data. However, projects, for which survey responses were obtained, appear to have more publications than the typical ATP intramural project. The average publication performance for ATP funded NIST projects may thus be no different from the typical NIST research project.

In addition to the analysis of the quantitative outputs and outcomes associated with intramural projects, qualitative information was collected in an effort to compare the nature of the intramural funded project with that of research activity that would have occurred in the absence of such funding. PIs reported that:

- In the absence of ATP funding, 54 percent of the projects would not have been undertaken. For 40 percent of these cases where the PI said that projects with similar goals and milestones would *not* have been undertaken without ATP funding, an alternative project would have been undertaken in the same broadly defined research area. A majority of these hypothetical projects in the same broad research area would have generated less new measurement technology and fewer new standards than did the ATP project.

- In the absence of ATP funding, 46 percent of the projects would have been undertaken with similar goals and milestones. However, these hypothetical projects without ATP support, although with similar goals and milestones, would have taken an estimated 12 months longer to complete, been less technically challenging, and generated fewer technical outputs, including technical papers, new measurement technology, new standards, and new databases.

In sum, in more than half the cases, similar projects would not have been undertaken in the absence of ATP support, and for the remaining 46 percent of projects where NIST would have had similar projects, the ATP-supported projects are perceived by the PIs to have outperformed the analogous projects that would have taken place without the ATP support.

## Response rates to the PI survey

During the FY 1992 through FY 2000 period, ATP funded 1,052 intramural projects. Two hundred and seventy eight (278) PIs who were at NIST at the time of the study and were associated with 510 of these projects received electronic surveys.

Surveys were returned with at least some information for one or more projects by 43 percent of the 278 PIs; surveys were returned with at least some information for 41 percent of the 510 projects. Table 4.1 summarizes the PI response rates by laboratory, and Table 4.2 summarizes the project

*Table 4.1* PI response rates to the survey, by laboratory (in percentages)

| Laboratory | Number of PIs | Response rate |
| --- | --- | --- |
| Electronics and Electrical Engineering (81) | 40 | 38 |
| Manufacturing Engineering (82) | 38 | 58 |
| Chemical Science and Technology (83) | 54 | 32 |
| Physics (84) | 36 | 53 |
| Material Science and Engineering (85) | 57 | 40 |
| Building and Fire Research (86) | 13 | 38 |
| Computer Systems (87) | 11 | 45 |
| Information Technology (89) | 29 | 48 |
| All | 278 | 43 |

*Table 4.2* Project response rates to the survey, by laboratory (in percentages)

| Laboratory | Number of projects | Response rate |
| --- | --- | --- |
| Electronics and Electrical Engineering (81) | 89 | 43 |
| Manufacturing Engineering (82) | 72 | 54 |
| Chemical Science and Technology (83) | 85 | 25 |
| Physics (84) | 68 | 49 |
| Material Science and Engineering (85) | 115 | 43 |
| Building and Fire Research (86) | 18 | 28 |
| Computer Systems (87) | 19 | 32 |
| Information Technology (89) | 44 | 41 |
| All | 510 | 41 |

Table 4.3 Project response rates to the survey, by year
of origination (in percentages)

| Fiscal year | Response rate |
|---|---|
| 1992 | 16 of 41 projects = 39.0 |
| 1993 | 15 of 40 projects = 37.5 |
| 1994 | 22 of 52 projects = 42.3 |
| 1995 | 30 of 66 projects = 45.5 |
| 1996 | 28 of 73 projects = 38.4 |
| 1997 | 19 of 52 projects = 36.5 |
| 1998 | 32 of 75 projects = 42.7 |
| 1999 | 29 of 65 projects = 44.6 |
| 2000 | 18 of 46 projects = 39.1 |
| All | 209 of 510 projects = 41.0 |

response rates by laboratory. In both tables, and in all tables that follow, laboratory 87 is retained as a separate laboratory although it was combined into laboratory 89 in 1997 and so reported above when summarizing budget allocations across laboratories. Of the 209 returned surveys, 30 reported that information was no longer available on the project; and thus, none of the survey questions was answered for those 30 projects. Table 4.3 shows the overall response rates, by the year of project origination.

The response rate differed for some questions; therefore, a probability of response model was estimated for each individual question. The probability of response to a question is hypothesized to be a function of the difficulty of responding, the age of the project, the project's budget, and laboratory effects. The difficulty (dif) of responding for the PI is measured by the number of intramural research awards that the PI received.[2] The age (age) of the project is measured by the number of years since the project began. The total budget (budget) of the project is measured in constant 1996 dollars.[3] The laboratory (lab81,...,lab89) of the funded PI is also held constant in the model:

Probability of response = $f$ (dif, age, budget, lab81, lab82, lab83,
lab84, lab85, lab86, lab87, lab89).

When appropriate, the probit results from the probability of response model are provided as each survey question is discussed.

The response models show that not all explanatory variables were important for response to all of the questions. However, for those questions where the explanatory variables for response were important, and controlling for the other variables that affect response, a PI was less likely to respond to a question for a particular project the greater the difficulty of responding and the greater the age of the project. In contrast, other things being controlled, response was more likely the larger the project's budget. The laboratory effects on the response probability, held constant in each response model, are at times significant as well.

## Project outputs and outcomes

Information was requested from each PI on broadly defined outputs from each research project. These outputs included the effect of ATP intramural funding on the scope of laboratory research, publications, citations, patents, presentations, and the leveraging effect on other funding sources. Each is discussed in order below.

### Scope of laboratory research

Regarding the effect of intramural funding on the scope of laboratory research, each PI was asked about the relationship of the intramural project to ongoing research in the laboratory. As shown in Table 4.4, 56.25 percent $(n = 176)^4$ of the projects initiated a new research direction, that is, they expanded NIST competencies in new areas as opposed to complementing an ongoing research agenda.

*Table 4.4* Effect of ATP intramural funding on the scope of laboratory research

| *Laboratory* | *Number of projects* | *Initiate new research direction (%)* |
|---|---|---|
| Electronics and Electrical Engineering (81) | 25 | 76 |
| Manufacturing Engineering (82) | 35 | 43 |
| Chemical Science and Technology (83) | 19 | 63 |
| Physics (84) | 29 | 55 |
| Material Science and Engineering (85) | 44 | 55 |
| Building and Fire Research (86) | 5 | 40 |
| Computer Systems (87) | 5 | 60 |
| Information Technology (89) | 14 | 57 |
| All | 176 | 56 |

Notes
Did the scope of this intramural research project complement an ongoing research agenda in your laboratory, or did it help to initiate a new research direction – that is, did it expand NIST's competencies in new areas? Please explain. Expanded scope = 1, otherwise = 0.

Table 4.5 shows the joint estimation of the probability of responding to the scope question and the probability of answering "Yes" to the question. Estimating jointly the probability of response and the probability that scope increased shows that the correlation of the disturbances for the two equations is positive and indeed almost equal to 1.0. When the error in the response model is large and response is more likely to occur, then the error

*Table 4.5* Probit model of scope with sample selection

| Model | Variable | Coefficient | Standard error | z | $P > |z|$ |
|-------|----------|-------------|----------------|-----|--------|
| Scope | age | −0.06360 | 0.02990 | −2.13 | 0.033 |
| | budget | 1.44E−06 | 3.93E−07 | 3.67 | 0.000 |
| | lab82 | −0.1503 | 0.2346 | −0.64 | 0.522 |
| | lab83 | −0.3794 | 0.2362 | −1.61 | 0.108 |
| | lab84 | 0.01499 | 0.2291 | 0.07 | 0.948 |
| | lab85 | −0.1499 | 0.2054 | −0.73 | 0.466 |
| | lab86 | −0.4835 | 0.4270 | −1.13 | 0.257 |
| | lab87 | −0.07728 | 0.3868 | −0.20 | 0.842 |
| | lab89 | −0.2905 | 0.2808 | −1.03 | 0.301 |
| | constant | −0.5794 | 0.2367 | −2.45 | 0.014 |
| Selection | dif | −0.07303 | 0.03643 | −2.00 | 0.045 |
| | age | −0.06444 | 0.02646 | −2.43 | 0.015 |
| | budget | 1.65E−06 | 3.99E−07 | 4.14 | 0.000 |
| | lab82 | 0.4847 | 0.2118 | 2.29 | 0.022 |
| | lab83 | −0.3150 | 0.2169 | −1.45 | 0.146 |
| | lab84 | 0.3584 | 0.2120 | 1.69 | 0.091 |
| | lab85 | 0.1915 | 0.1894 | 1.01 | 0.312 |
| | lab86 | −0.1358 | 0.3525 | −0.39 | 0.700 |
| | lab87 | 0.003369 | 0.3465 | 0.01 | 0.992 |
| | lab89 | −0.1509 | 0.2567 | −0.59 | 0.557 |
| | constant | −0.2003 | 0.2319 | −0.86 | 0.388 |
| | athrho | 4.5125 | 56.8739 | 0.08 | 0.937 |
| | $\rho$ | 0.9998 | 0.02738 | — | — |

Number of observations = 510             Log likelihood = −419.9873
Censored observations = 334               Wald $\chi^2(9) = 20.40$
Uncensored observations = 176             Prob $> \chi^2 = 0.0156$
LR test of independent equations ($\rho = 0$): $\chi^2(1) = 3.07$; Prob $> \chi^2 = 0.0798$

Notes
The results are for the joint maximum likelihood estimation of the probit model for scope and the response (selection) model for the 176 respondents that provided answers to the scope question. The statistic athrho is inverse hyperbolic tangent of $\rho$ the correlation between the disturbances in the probit model for scope and in the selection model for response to the scope question. Here and in the subsequent tables, $E + nn$ or $E − nn$ means multiply by 10 to the + or −nn power.

*Table 4.6* Predicted effect of ATP intramural funding on the scope of laboratory research

| Laboratory | Number of projects | Probability initiate new research direction (%) |
|---|---|---|
| Electronics and Electrical Engineering (81) | 89 | 22 |
| Manufacturing Engineering (82) | 72 | 21 |
| Chemical Science and Technology (83) | 85 | 14 |
| Physics (84) | 68 | 24 |
| Material Science and Engineering (85) | 115 | 20 |
| Building and Fire Research (86) | 18 | 12 |
| Computer Systems (87) | 19 | 17 |
| Information Technology (89) | 44 | 19 |
| All | 510 | 20 |

Notes
The probability that the intramural research project initiated a new research direction as predicted by the model reported in Table 4.5: average of the probabilities predicted for each project in the categories shown.

in the probit model for scope is also large and scope is more likely to have increased. For that reason, after controlling for the response bias in the results, the percentages in Table 4.4 showing new research directions tend to be overestimates of the true probability that the laboratories' intramural projects increased the scope of the laboratory research.

Table 4.6 shows the response-adjusted probabilities as predicted by the maximum likelihood estimates of the probit model for scope and the probit model from response.[5] The model's estimates are shown in Table 4.5, and from that model the probability of a "Yes" answer to the scope question is predicted for each observation in the complete 510 project sample.[6] The predictions are averaged for each laboratory to get the results shown in Table 4.6. On average, 20 percent of the projects are perceived to have an increase in scope (last row and column of Table 4.6). Perhaps reflecting the 1997 ATP policy shift of intramural funding emphasis to generic projects that could cut across a group of ATP projects, older projects are less likely to be perceived as increasing the scope of the laboratory's research.

## Publications

Information was requested on the number of publications, either in print or accepted for publication and forthcoming that resulted directly from each project. Of the 179 projects, the mean number of publications per project

*Table 4.7* Publications per project resulting from ATP intramural projects

| Laboratory | Number of projects | Mean number of publications | Range of publications |
|---|---|---|---|
| Electronics and Electrical Engineering (81) | 25 | 4.0 | 0–11 |
| Manufacturing Engineering (82) | 35 | 3.7 | 1–17 |
| Chemical Science and Technology (83) | 19 | 6.7 | 0–61 |
| Physics (84) | 28 | 4.3 | 0–18 |
| Material Science and Engineering (85) | 47 | 7.8 | 0–62 |
| Building and Fire Research (86) | 5 | 1.8 | 0–4 |
| Computer Systems (87) | 5 | 1.6 | 0–5 |
| Information Technology (89) | 15 | 2.3 | 0–7 |
| All | 179 | 5.0 | 0–62 |

Notes
Please provide complete bibliographic citations for all technical papers that resulted from this project and were published in professional journals, conference proceedings, or elsewhere.

was 5.01; the range was 0–62 as shown in Table 4.7.[7] Also shown in Table 4.7 are the mean and range by laboratory.

The probit model for response to the question about publications is in Table 4.8, and the results show that the probability of responding decreases with difficulty and with age, but increases with budget. The model shown in Table 4.8 is also exactly the probit model for response to the questions about citations and about patents, because the respondents to all three questions were the same. Citations and patents are discussed subsequently.

A complete negative binomial ("count") maximum likelihood regression model for the number of publications reported for each project can be readily estimated. However, when estimated as a single equation, one does not know whether the effects of the explanatory variables on the estimated number of publications reflect true explanatory effects for the population of ATP projects, or instead reflect the association of the variables with the probability of response which is then in turn associated with the number of publications. To address this problem, the negative binomial model for publications was estimated simultaneously with the probit model for selection into the sample (i.e. the model for the probability of response to the question about publications).[8] It is for some models very difficult to get maximum likelihood estimates of the response model and the count model of publications to converge; indeed, convergence and hence the

*Table 4.8* Probit model for response to the publication question

| Variable | Coefficient | Standard error | z | P > \|z\| | Mean of X |
|---|---|---|---|---|---|
| constant | −2.3555 | 0.7365 | −3.198 | 0.0014 | — |
| dif | −0.7223E−01 | 0.4397E−01 | −1.643 | 0.1004 | 2.5882 |
| age | −0.4449E−01 | 0.2714E−01 | −1.639 | 0.1012 | 5.7510 |
| ln budget | 0.1999 | 0.5962E−01 | 3.353 | 0.0008 | 11.44970 |
| lab82 | 0.5094 | 0.2098 | 2.428 | 0.0152 | 0.1412 |
| lab83 | −0.3268 | 0.2177 | −1.501 | 0.1333 | 0.1667 |
| lab84 | 0.3112 | 0.2119 | 1.469 | 0.1419 | 0.1333 |
| lab85 | 0.2427 | 0.1876 | 1.294 | 0.1956 | 0.2255 |
| lab86 | −0.1646 | 0.3544 | −0.464 | 0.6424 | 0.3529E−01 |
| lab87 | −0.6721E−01 | 0.3471 | −0.194 | 0.8465 | 0.3725E−01 |
| lab89 | −0.7373E−01 | 0.2533 | −0.291 | 0.7710 | 0.8627E−01 |

Number of observations = 510    Log likelihood function = −310.9411
Restricted log likelihood = −330.5062    $\chi^2$ = 39.13034
Degrees of freedom = 10    Prob[$\chi^2$ > value] = 0.00002409
Measures of fit: Estrella = 0.07604; McFadden = 0.05920

estimates are available only for a very parsimonious count model for publications. That parsimonious model, estimated simultaneously with the full response model, is the only model of publications that is of interest or importance here. That is because we have the descriptive statistics for the reported publications as shown in Table 4.7. A fully specified single-equation negative binomial count model provides a good fit to those data for the 179 projects that responded, but we do not care about that model because it confounds response effects with the effects of underlying explanatory variables. If we want to have the descriptive statistics for the 179 reporting projects, we have Table 4.7, while if we want to estimate what the publications were for an ATP intramural project in the population, we need to use the best model that is estimable simultaneously with the model for response.

With correction for selection into the sample, Table 4.9 shows the negative binomial count model for publications that could be estimated with the data available for the sample of ATP intramural projects. The estimated number of publications increases with the natural logarithm of the budget, and laboratory 82 is expected to have fewer publications holding constant the effect of the budget (the model actually predicts slightly higher publications per project for the 72 projects in laboratory 82 once the effect of budget size is included). Simultaneously estimated with the negative binomial count model, the individual coefficients in the model

*Table 4.9* Negative binomial regression model for the number of publications from a project, with correction for sample selection

| Variable | Coefficient | Standard error | z | $P > |z|$ | Mean of X |
|---|---|---|---|---|---|
| constant | −10.5813 | 1.4514 | −7.290 | 0.0000 | — |
| ln budget | 0.8635 | 0.1126 | 7.671 | 0.0000 | 11.6859 |
| lab82 | −0.1590 | 0.2735 | −0.581 | 0.5611 | 0.1955 |
| Overdispersion parameter for negative binomial | | | | | |
| $\theta$ | 0.2272 | 0.1215 | 1.870 | 0.0615 | — |
| Standard deviation of heterogeneity | | | | | |
| $\sigma$ | 1.5611 | 0.2014 | 7.753 | 0.0000 | — |
| Correlation of heterogeneity and selection | | | | | |
| $\rho$ | 0.9999999994 | 0.6184 | 1.617 | 0.1058 | — |

Number of observations = 510          Log likelihood function = −746.3022
Restricted log likelihood = −1210.219     $\chi^2 = 927.8335$
Degrees of freedom = 2               Prob[$\chi^2$ > value] = 0.0000000
Mean of LHS variable = 5.00559        Restricted Log $L$ is Poisson +
Log $L$ for initial probit = −310.9411      Probit (indep)
Means for Psn/Neg.Bin. use selected data   Log $L$ for initial Poisson = −899.2779

of response are no longer significant, but they are in themselves not of interest to us. The maximum likelihood correlation coefficient between the error in the probit model of response and in the count model is almost 1.0. From the estimated coefficients in the negative binomial model as corrected for sample selection, we have the predicted number of publications for a project equal to:

exp(−10.58 + 0.8635 ln budget − 0.1590 lab82).

Following this formulation, Table 4.10 uses the negative binomial model (eliminating the selection effect) to predict the number of publications for each of the 510 projects in the complete sample. Table 4.10 shows the average predictions which, because of the elimination of the selection bias, show fewer predicted publications as compared to the actual numbers of publications per project for those responding to the survey. The model's prediction is that on average for all of the 510 projects, there were about two publications for every three projects (0.69 publications per project), rather than five publications per project as suggested by the respondents to the survey. To provide an indication of the robustness of the prediction here, we also estimated the negative binomial model with control for sample

*Table 4.10* Predicted publications per project resulting from ATP intramural projects

| Laboratory | Number of projects | Mean number of publications | Range of publications |
|---|---|---|---|
| Manufacturing Engineering (82) | 72 | 0.7 | 0.05–4.9 |
| All except Manufacturing Engineering (82) | 438 | 0.7 | 0.3–6.7 |
| All | 510 | 0.7 | 0.05–6.7 |

selection by using a two-step method directly analogous to the well-known model of Heckman. The model as we estimated it does not face the difficulties of obtaining convergence that occur with the full information maximum likelihood estimation of the selection and count models simultaneously. As a result, all of the explanatory variables other than the identifying variable, dif, could be included in the count model. Instead of predicting 0.69 publications per project, the two-step model predicts 0.65 publications per project – essentially the same answer of about two publications for every three projects.[9] However, our alternative approach is less orthodox than the formal approach using Greene's full information maximum likelihood approach, and we present only those results here.

## Citations

The number of citations of each in-print publication was calculated on the basis of information in the Expanded Science Citation Index, as accessed through the Web of Science. Each publication that a PI reported on his/her returned survey was verified in the Expanded Science Citation Index and the number of non-self (including all co-authors) citations was counted. The mean ($n = 133$) number of non-self citations per publication for those projects reporting publications was 1.66; the range was 0–33 (see Table 4.11).

The probit model for response to the citations question is identical to the model for response in Table 4.8, because the respondents to the two questions were the same. Table 4.12 shows the negative binomial model for the counts of citations per project with correction for sample selection. The procedure used is the same as described in the section about the count model of publications.

The model was used to predict the number of citations for each of the 510 projects, and taking that prediction and then dividing by the number of publications for each project, Table 4.13 shows the average predictions per publication for the typical project with the characteristics of the

*Table 4.11* Citations per in-print publication resulting from ATP intramural projects

| Laboratory | Number of projects | Mean number of citations | Range of citations |
|---|---|---|---|
| Electronics and Electrical Engineering (81) | 18 | 0.2 | 1–1.3 |
| Manufacturing Engineering (82) | 23 | 0.1 | 0–1.6 |
| Chemical Science and Technology (83) | 15 | 1.2 | 0–4.6 |
| Physics (84) | 21 | 5.2 | 0–33 |
| Material Science and Engineering (85) | 39 | 2.3 | 0–32.7 |
| Building and Fire Research (86) | 3 | 0.0 | — |
| Computer Systems (87) | 3 | 0.2 | 0–0.5 |
| Information Technology (89) | 11 | 0.1 | 0–0.5 |
| All | 133 | 1.7 | 0–33 |

133 projects reporting publications. The predicted number of citations per project is:

$$\exp(-11.18 + 0.4695 \text{ age} + 0.4560 \ln \text{budget} + 3.40 \text{ lab83} + 3.96 \text{ lab84} + 2.43 \text{ lab85}).$$

For all projects having publications, the average number of citations is predicted to be about the same as the one and two-thirds citations per publication for the responding projects. Typical projects would have fewer publications and fewer citations, but the citations per publication would be about the same as for the reporting projects.

*Patents*

Patenting is not an integral part of the research mission of NIST scientists. However, a few PIs for selected projects did report that a patent had either been filed or had been received. As shown in Table 4.14, on average ($n = 179$), the number of patents per project was 0.05 with a range of 0–3. Disaggregation of the survey data by laboratory is not meaningful for this output measure because so few patents had been filed or received; for the same reason, estimating a count model for patents is not sensible.

*Presentations*

Presentations are the primary mode for quickly and effectively disseminating information from NIST research. On average ($n = 174$), the number

*Table 4.12* Negative binomial regression model for the number of citations per project, with correction for sample selection

| Model | Variable | Coefficient | Standard error | z | P > |z| | Mean of X |
|---|---|---|---|---|---|---|
| Negative binomial | constant | -11.1785 | 1.5215 | -7.347 | 0.0000 | — |
| | age | 0.4695 | 0.5978E-01 | 7.854 | 0.0000 | 5.4022 |
| | ln budget | 0.4560 | 0.1062 | 4.292 | 0.0000 | 11.6859 |
| | lab83 | 3.4042 | 0.4749 | 7.169 | 0.0000 | 0.1061 |
| | lab84 | 3.9578 | 0.4772 | 8.294 | 0.0000 | 0.1564 |
| | lab85 | 2.4298 | 0.4204 | 5.780 | 0.0000 | 0.2626 |
| Selection | constant | -2.3697 | 0.7311 | -3.241 | 0.0012 | — |
| | dif | -0.7404E-01 | 0.5028E-01 | -1.473 | 0.1409 | 2.5882 |
| | age | -0.4296E-01 | 0.2898E-01 | -1.482 | 0.1383 | 5.7510 |
| | ln budget | 0.2001 | 0.5943E-01 | 3.367 | 0.0008 | 11.4497 |
| | lab82 | 0.5248 | 0.2119 | 2.477 | 0.0133 | 0.1412 |
| | lab83 | -0.3151 | 0.2317 | -1.360 | 0.1739 | 0.1667 |
| | lab84 | 0.3240 | 0.2125 | 1.525 | 0.1273 | 0.1333 |
| | lab85 | 0.2433 | 0.1885 | 1.291 | 0.1969 | 0.2255 |
| | lab86 | -0.1455 | 0.3511 | -0.414 | 0.6786 | 0.3529E-01 |
| | lab87 | -0.5030E-01 | 0.3488 | -0.144 | 0.8853 | 0.3725E-01 |
| | lab89 | -0.6848E-01 | 0.2595 | -0.264 | 0.7919 | 0.8627E-01 |
| Overdispersion parameter for negative binomial | $\theta$ | 0.8947E-01 | 0.3696E-01 | 2.421 | 0.0155 | — |
| Standard deviation of heterogeneity | $\sigma$ | 2.1222 | 0.1493 | 14.214 | 0.0000 | — |
| Correlation of heterogeneity and selection | $\rho$ | 0.1249 | 0.1456 | 0.858 | 0.3907 | — |

Number of observations = 510
$\chi^2$ = 4160.058
Mean of LHS variable = 10.2905
Log $L$ for initial Poisson = -2402.5950

Log likelihood function = -633.5072
Degrees of freedom = 2
Restricted Log $L$ is Poisson + Probit (indep)
Means for Psn/Neg.Bin. use selected data

Restricted log likelihood = -2713.536
Prob[$\chi^2$ > value] = 0.0000000
Log $L$ for initial probit = -310.9411

*Table 4.13* Predicted citations per predicted publication from ATP intramural projects, with correction for selection, for the 133 projects reporting at least one publication

| Laboratory | Number of projects | Mean number of citations per publication | Range of citations per publication |
|---|---|---|---|
| All | 133 | 1.8 | 0.01–22.9 |

Notes
The count model for publications with correction for sample selection predicts an average of 1.00 publication for the 133 projects for which actual publications were 5.01 per project. The error in the selection model was highly correlated with the error in the publications count model, so the 133 reporting projects had more publications than expected for the typical projects with their characteristics. The count model for citations with correction for sample selection predicts an average of 1.48 citations for the 133 projects. The ratio of the predicted citations to the predicted publications averaged across the 133 projects is 1.76. The reporting projects had more publications than expected for the typical project and somewhat more citations; the ratio, or citations per publication, for the typical project with publications is essentially the same as for the 133 reporting projects.

*Table 4.14* Patents per project from the ATP intramural projects

| Laboratory | Number of projects reporting | Mean number of patents | Range of patents |
|---|---|---|---|
| All | 179 | 0.05 | 0–3 |

*Table 4.15* Presentations per project resulting from ATP intramural projects

| Laboratory | Number of projects | Mean number of presentations | Range of presentations |
|---|---|---|---|
| Electronics and Electrical Engineering (81) | 25 | 4.2 | 0–15 |
| Manufacturing Engineering (82) | 34 | 7.9 | 0–60 |
| Chemical Science and Technology (83) | 19 | 17.3 | 0–150 |
| Physics (84) | 28 | 7.6 | 0–40 |
| Material Science and Engineering (85) | 43 | 15.4 | 0–150 |
| Building and Fire Research (86) | 5 | 3.4 | 0–10 |
| Computer Systems (87) | 5 | 2.6 | 0–10 |
| Information Technology (89) | 15 | 3.4 | 0–9 |
| All | 174 | 9.6 | 0–150 |

Note
Approximately, how many professional presentations (outside of NIST) related to this project have been given?

of presentations per project was 9.55 with a range of 0–150 (see Table 4.15). The probit model for response to the presentations question is shown in Table 4.16. Table 4.17 shows the negative binomial model estimated simultaneously with the model for response following the procedure introduced to model publications above. The model was used to predict the number of presentations for each of the 510 projects as the base to the natural logarithms raised to the power:

$$-11.32 + 0.9177 \ln \text{budget} + 0.5885 \text{ lab82} + 0.5774 \text{ lab83}$$
$$+ 1.007 \text{ lab84} + 0.1414 \text{ lab85} + 0.1303 \text{ lab86} - 1.013 \text{ lab87}$$
$$+ 0.3731 \text{ lab89}.$$

Table 4.18 shows the average prediction per project for each laboratory after correcting for the response effect. About one presentation per project is expected on average for all 510 projects, rather than almost 10 presentations per project for those responding to the survey. Again, it is worth noting that the result is the same result we obtained initially using a two-step estimator analogous to Heckman's estimator. That model predicted 0.90 presentations per project as compared to the prediction here of 1.01 – essentially one presentation per project.

*Table 4.16* Probit model of response to presentation question

| Variable | Coefficient | Standard error | z | $P > |z|$ | Mean of X |
|---|---|---|---|---|---|
| constant | −2.2814 | 0.7388 | −3.088 | 0.0020 | — |
| dif | −0.9528E−01 | 0.4459E−01 | −2.137 | 0.0326 | 2.5882 |
| age | −0.4515E−01 | 0.2721E−01 | −1.659 | 0.0971 | 5.7510 |
| ln budget | 0.2000 | 0.5993E−01 | 3.337 | 0.0008 | 11.4497 |
| lab82 | 0.4639 | 0.2099 | 2.210 | 0.0271 | 0.1412 |
| lab83 | −0.3531 | 0.2180 | −1.620 | 0.1053 | 0.1667 |
| lab84 | 0.3026 | 0.2120 | 1.427 | 0.1535 | 0.1333 |
| lab85 | 0.1392 | 0.1889 | 0.737 | 0.4613 | 0.2255 |
| lab86 | −0.1956 | 0.3550 | −0.551 | 0.5816 | 0.3529E−01 |
| lab87 | −0.8796E−01 | 0.3479 | −0.253 | 0.8004 | 0.3725E−01 |
| lab89 | −0.1013 | 0.2539 | −0.399 | 0.6898 | 0.8627E−01 |

Number of observations = 510           Log likelihood function = −307.9056
Restricted log likelihood = −327.3245     $\chi^2 = 38.8378$
Degrees of freedom = 10                 Prob[$\chi^2 >$ value] = 0.2710E−04
Fit measures: Estrella = 0.07550; McFadden = 0.05933

*Table 4.17* Negative binomial regression model for the number of presentations per project, with correction for sample selection

| Variable | Coefficient | Standard error | z | $P > |z|$ | Mean of X |
|---|---|---|---|---|---|
| constant | −11.3196 | 0.8405 | −13.467 | 0.0000 | |
| ln budget | 0.9177 | 0.6440E−01 | 14.251 | 0.0000 | 11.6872 |
| lab82 | 0.5885 | 0.2192 | 2.684 | 0.0073 | 0.1954 |
| lab83 | 0.5774 | 0.2163 | 2.669 | 0.0076 | 0.1092 |
| lab84 | 1.0069 | 0.2592 | 3.884 | 0.0001 | 0.1609 |
| lab85 | 0.1414 | 0.2058 | 0.687 | 0.4921 | 0.2471 |
| lab86 | 0.1303 | 0.4035 | 0.323 | 0.7467 | 0.2874E−01 |
| lab87 | −1.0129 | 0.9033 | −1.121 | 0.2622 | 0.2874E−01 |
| lab89 | 0.3731 | 0.3363 | 1.109 | 0.2674 | 0.8621E−01 |

Overdispersion parameter for negative binomial
| | | | | | |
|---|---|---|---|---|---|
| $\theta$ | 0.5007E−01 | 0.1794E−01 | 2.791 | 0.0053 | |

Standard deviation of heterogeneity
| | | | | | |
|---|---|---|---|---|---|
| $\sigma$ | 1.6187 | 0.7094E−01 | 22.818 | 0.0000 | |

Correlation of heterogeneity and selection
| | | | | | |
|---|---|---|---|---|---|
| $\rho$ | 0.9999999998 | 0.1166 | 8.574 | 0.0000 | |

Number of observations = 510                Log likelihood function = −795.8038
Restricted log likelihood = −2030.521        $\chi^2$ = 2469.434
Degrees of freedom = 2                       Prob[$\chi^2$ > value] = 0.0000000
Mean of LHS variable = 9.5345                Restricted Log $L$ is Poisson +
Log $L$ for initial probit = −307.9056          Probit (indep)
Means for Psn/Neg.Bin. use selected data     Log $L$ for initial Poisson = −1722.6152

*Table 4.18* Predicted presentations per project resulting from ATP intramural projects

| Laboratory | Number of projects | Mean number of presentations | Range of presentations |
|---|---|---|---|
| All | 510 | 1 | 0.02–10.6 |

### Leveraging additional funding

In addition to the knowledge spillovers associated with publications, citations, and presentations, the ATP intramural projects also leveraged other sources of funding such as NIST competency awards or CRADA activity. For the responding projects ($n = 176$), 30.68 percent of the projects leveraged additional funding as shown in Table 4.19.

*Table 4.19* Impact of ATP intramural project on leveraging other sources of funding

| Laboratory | Number of projects | Leveraging rate (%) |
|---|---|---|
| Electronics and Electrical Engineering (81) | 25 | 24 |
| Manufacturing Engineering (82) | 35 | 20 |
| Chemical Science and Technology (83) | 18 | 39 |
| Physics (84) | 27 | 44 |
| Material Science and Engineering (85) | 47 | 34 |
| Building and Fire Research (86) | 5 | 20 |
| Computer Systems (87) | 5 | 20 |
| Information Technology (89) | 14 | 29 |
| All | 176 | 31 |

Note
Did this project contribute to the basis for subsequent NIST competency awards, other sources of federal funding to the laboratory, or CRADA activity? Yes = 1, No = 0.

Table 4.20 presents the maximum likelihood estimation of the probit model with sample selection.[10] Although the model of selection (response) is quite significant and tells the same story we have already seen about response, there are not significant differences across the laboratories in the probability of leveraging subsequent competency awards. The differences not being significant, we report for the 510 projects in the complete sample simply the average prediction of that probability for a project. That average probability is 0.14 and the range across the 510 projects for the predicted probability of leveraging is from 0.02 to 0.37. However, we cannot reject the possibility that the selection and leveraging models are independent, and so perhaps the estimates from our respondents in Table 4.19 are the best ones.

## NIST benchmarks

To place these outputs and impacts in perspective, ATP provided selected NIST-wide benchmark data. As shown in Table 4.21, the performance of the ATP-funded projects that reported their publications in response to the survey had a much higher number of publications per million dollars of budget (in constant 1996 dollars) than the average project in the same NIST laboratory. The estimated models of response and of publications do suggest that the responding ATP-funded projects performed exceptionally well relative to all ATP intramural projects. If the predictions

*Table 4.20* Probit model of leveraging competency awards or similar funded awards with sample selection

| Model | Variable | Coefficient | Standard error | z | P > \|z\| |
|---|---|---|---|---|---|
| Competency | age | 0.03821 | 0.06000 | 0.64 | 0.524 |
| | ln budget | 0.2448 | 0.1021 | 2.40 | 0.017 |
| | lab82 | −0.001761 | 0.3903 | −0.00 | 0.996 |
| | lab83 | 0.1585 | 0.4583 | 0.35 | 0.729 |
| | lab84 | 0.4983 | 0.3429 | 1.45 | 0.146 |
| | lab85 | 0.3291 | 0.3013 | 1.09 | 0.275 |
| | lab86 | −0.1419 | 0.6127 | −0.23 | 0.817 |
| | lab87 | −0.3292 | 0.6559 | −0.50 | 0.616 |
| | lab89 | 0.1645 | 0.4259 | 0.39 | 0.699 |
| | constant | −4.3372 | 1.3162 | −3.30 | 0.001 |
| Selection | dif | −0.06362 | 0.04311 | −1.48 | 0.140 |
| | age | −0.06627 | 0.02703 | −2.45 | 0.014 |
| | budget | 1.60E−06 | 4.01E−07 | 3.98 | 0.000 |
| | lab82 | 0.4850 | 0.2129 | 2.28 | 0.023 |
| | lab83 | −0.3567 | 0.2214 | −1.61 | 0.107 |
| | lab84 | 0.2831 | 0.2150 | 1.32 | 0.188 |
| | lab85 | 0.2592 | 0.1892 | 1.37 | 0.171 |
| | lab86 | −0.1488 | 0.3539 | −0.42 | 0.674 |
| | lab87 | 0.01510 | 0.3485 | 0.04 | 0.965 |
| | lab89 | −0.1433 | 0.2568 | −0.56 | 0.577 |
| | constant | −0.2059 | 0.2388 | −0.86 | 0.389 |
| | athrho | 0.7822 | 1.0993 | 0.71 | 0.477 |
| | $\rho$ | 0.6540 | 0.6292 | | |

Number of observations = 510          Censored observations = 334
Uncensored observations = 176          Log likelihood = −407.6357
Wald $\chi^2(9)$ = 12.66          Prob > $\chi^2$ = 0.1788
LR test of independent equations ($\rho$ = 0): $\chi^2(1)$ = 0.68; Prob > $\chi^2$ = 0.4107

of the model of publications with control for selection effects were used instead of the actual performance of the ATP-funded projects that responded to the survey, the predicted publications per million dollars of budget for the ATP intramural projects would not outperform the typical NIST projects. The predictions, however, are not the actual performance observed, but rather would be the best guess about the performance of an analogous, hypothetical project apart from random error. On average, the actual performance regarding publications for the reporting ATP intramural projects far exceeded the performance of the typical NIST laboratory projects.

*Table 4.21* Comparison of publications for ATP intramural and NIST projects

| Laboratory | n | Publications | Budget (1996 $s) | Publications per $M of budget |
|---|---|---|---|---|
| *ATP intramural projects with starting dates from FY 1994–2000 and respondents with publications and budget data* | | | | |
| Electronics and Electrical Engineering (81) | 24 | 93 | 2,983 K | 31.2 |
| Manufacturing Engineering (82) | 29 | 100 | 7,015 K | 14.3 |
| Chemical Science and Technology (83) | 17 | 67 | 4,223 K | 15.9 |
| Physics (84) | 20 | 72 | 3,623 K | 19.9 |
| Material Science and Engineering (85) | 44 | 352 | 6,613 K | 53.2 |
| Building and Fire Research (86) | 4 | 9 | 644 K | 14.0 |
| Information Technology (89) | 17 | 38 | 2,771 K | 14.0 |

| | Average annual publications | Average annual budget (1996 $s) | Publications per $M of budget |
|---|---|---|---|
| *All NIST laboratories from FY 1994–2000* | | | |
| Electronics and Electrical Engineering (81) | 232 | 36,884 K | 6.3 |
| Manufacturing Engineering (82) | 163 | 28,779 K | 5.70 |
| Chemical Science and Technology (83) | 350 | 41,127 K | 8.5 |
| Physics (84) | 276 | 29,920 K | 9.2 |
| Material Science and Engineering (85) | 489 | 41,792 K | 11.7 |
| Building and Fire Research (86) | 241 | 20,856 K | 11.6 |
| Information Technology (89) | 197 | 40,703 K | 4.8 |

Notes

K denotes thousands, and M denotes millions. The 510 observation sample of ATP intramural projects includes projects as old as those beginning in FY 1992 (with age 2002–1992 = 10) and as young as those beginning in FY 2000 (with age 2002–2000 = 2). NIST provided budget data for each lab for FY 1994 through FY 2001, as well as publications data by lab for those years, for the years before, and for FY 2002. To have comparable data, in the table we used (1) ATP projects between 2 and 8 years old (the youngest starting in FY 2000 and the oldest starting in FY 1994), and (2) the NIST lab data for FY 1994 through FY 2000. As the estimated models (both the Greene approach and the *ad hoc* two-step approach) show, age is not a factor explaining publications *in the sample* where the youngest projects are 2 years old. For applied science and technology, the papers come fairly quickly. The publications and budgets for the ATP intramural projects are observed at the project level, and the matching is therefore exact. For the NIST lab performance, the publications and budget data are at the lab level. The appropriate lag between project funding and publications is not known, and further-more the projects extend over multiple years with publications coming throughout the projects' lives. Examination of the annual publications and budget (in constant 1996 dollars) data suggest a stable, annual relation between publications and budget, so for the NIST perform-ance results the average annual number of publications per million dollars of budget was used.

## Hypothetical effects of intramural funding

In an effort to compare the nature of the intramural funded project to research activities that would have occurred in the absence of such funding, a number of hypothetical questions were asked.

Overall ($n = 151$), PIs reported that 46 percent of the projects would have been undertaken as a project with similar goals and milestones had ATP funding not been received (see Table 4.22). However, these hypothetical projects, although with similar goals and milestones, would have taken longer to complete, would have been less technically challenging, and would have generated fewer technical outputs as noted below.

The probit model for undertaking similar projects absent ATP funding shows that neither project age nor project budget has a significant effect on the probability that a similar project will be undertaken. Table 4.23 shows the appropriate probit model with control for selection into the sample. For completeness and to allow comparison with Table 4.22, Table 4.24 uses the model to predict the probability that similar projects will be undertaken. However, as Table 4.23 shows, we cannot reject the hypothesis that the selection model is independent of the probit model regarding undertaking similar projects. Of course, the predicted probabilities in Table 4.24 are higher than those observed without control for sample selection, because the error in the probit for response is negatively correlated with the error in the probit for undertaking similar

*Table 4.22* Probability of undertaking a similar research project absent ATP intramural funding

| Laboratory | Number of projects | Probability (%) |
|---|---|---|
| Electronics and Electrical Engineering (81) | 20 | 40 |
| Manufacturing Engineering (82) | 30 | 50 |
| Chemical Science and Technology (83) | 16 | 44 |
| Physics (84) | 23 | 74 |
| Material Science and Engineering (85) | 42 | 45 |
| Building and Fire Research (86) | 3 | 33 |
| Computer Systems (87) | 3 | 0 |
| Information Technology (89) | 14 | 21 |
| All | 151 | 46 |

Notes
If you had not received funding for this ATP intramural project, would you have undertaken a project with similar goals and milestones? Yes = 1, No = 0. When making this comparison, please consider a hypothetical project with an amount of funding comparable to your ATP intramural project.

*Table 4.23* Probit model for undertaking similar project absent ATP funding with sample selection

| Model | Variable | Coefficient | Standard error | z | P > \|z\| |
|-------|----------|-------------|----------------|-----|---------|
| Absent | age | 0.03628 | 0.1318 | 0.28 | 0.783 |
| | budget | −1.11E−07 | 2.04E−06 | −0.05 | 0.957 |
| | lab82 | 0.03048 | 1.0092 | 0.03 | 0.976 |
| | lab83 | 0.1297 | 0.4068 | 0.32 | 0.750 |
| | lab84 | 0.7105 | 1.2128 | 0.59 | 0.558 |
| | lab85 | 0.01571 | 0.7380 | 0.02 | 0.983 |
| | lab86 | −0.01739 | 0.8894 | −0.02 | 0.984 |
| | lab89 | −0.5022 | 0.4946 | −1.02 | 0.310 |
| | constant | 0.2074 | 2.3398 | 0.09 | 0.929 |
| Selection | dif | −0.04750 | 0.05005 | −0.95 | 0.343 |
| | age | −0.08101 | 0.02883 | −2.81 | 0.005 |
| | budget | 1.61E−06 | 4.04E−07 | 3.98 | 0.000 |
| | lab82 | 0.4632 | 0.2291 | 2.02 | 0.043 |
| | lab83 | −0.2736 | 0.2301 | −1.19 | 0.234 |
| | lab84 | 0.2919 | 0.2208 | 1.32 | 0.186 |
| | lab85 | 0.3024 | 0.1994 | 1.52 | 0.129 |
| | lab86 | −0.3729 | 0.3980 | −0.94 | 0.349 |
| | lab89 | 0.01709 | 0.2610 | 0.07 | 0.948 |
| | constant | −0.3381 | 0.2484 | −1.36 | 0.173 |
| | athrho | −0.5433 | 2.5149 | −0.22 | 0.829 |
| | $\rho$ | −0.4955 | 1.897 | | |

Number of observations = 491   Censored observations = 343
Uncensored observations = 148   Log likelihood = −373.1646
Wald $\chi^2(8)$ = 9.74   Prob > $\chi^2$ = 0.2841
LR test of independent equations ($\rho = 0$): $\chi^2(1)$ = 0.03; Prob > $\chi^2$ = 0.8596

Note
The category lab87 predicts perfectly that there will be no such similar projects absent the ATP funding; it is therefore dropped from the model along with the 19 projects from lab87.

projects absent ATP funding. If one accepts the correlation estimated, then when the error in the response equation is large and a project is likely to respond, the error in the probit for undertaking similar projects is small and the reported project is less likely to have undertaken a similar project without the ATP support. However, the correlation is not at all significant, and the results from our respondents in Table 4.22 are the ones to use.

Table 4.25 shows that as a result of ATP funding, 84 percent of the research that was conducted was ahead in achieving similar goals and milestones by an average of 12 months ($n = 69$).

*Table 4.24* Predicted probability of undertaking a similar research project absent ATP intramural funding

| Laboratory | Number of projects | Probability (%) |
|---|---|---|
| Electronics and Electrical Engineering (81) | 89 | 70 |
| Manufacturing Engineering (82) | 72 | 70 |
| Chemical Science and Technology (83) | 85 | 70 |
| Physics (84) | 68 | 90 |
| Material Science and Engineering (85) | 115 | 70 |
| Building and Fire Research (86) | 18 | 60 |
| Computer Systems (87) | 19 | — |
| Information Technology (89) | 44 | 40 |

*Table 4.25* Effect of ATP intramural funding in achieving similar goals and milestones

| Laboratory | Number of projects | Ahead (%) | Months ahead | Same place (%) | Behind (%) |
|---|---|---|---|---|---|
| Electronics and Electrical Engineering (81) | 8 | 100 | 11 | 0 | 0 |
| Manufacturing Engineering (82) | 15 | 87 | 15 | 7 | 7 |
| Chemical Science and Technology (83) | 7 | 71 | 14 | 29 | 0 |
| Physics (84) | 17 | 100 | 10 | 0 | 0 |
| Material Science and Engineering (85) | 18 | 67 | 13 | 28 | 6 |
| Building and Fire Research (86) | 1 | 100 | 12 | 0 | 0 |
| Computer Systems (87) | 0 | — | — | — | — |
| Information Technology (89) | 3 | 67 | 9 | 33 | 0 |
| All | 69 | 84 | 12 | 13 | 3 |

Notes
For those who would have undertaken a project with similar goals and milestones absent ATP intramural funding. As a result of ATP funding, are you ahead/in the same place/behind in achieving similar goals and milestones? If ahead, by approximately how many months?

Table 4.26 shows the probit model for being ahead of schedule because of ATP funding (see Table 4.25) with control for the response to the question. The model for being ahead could not be estimated with age included (there were numerical problems and the model would not converge).

*Table 4.26* Probit model with control for response for being ahead of schedule

| Model | Variable | Coefficient | Standard error | z | P > \|z\| |
|---|---|---|---|---|---|
| Q10 ahead | ln budget | 0.2344 | 0.08814 | 2.66 | 0.008 |
| | lab83 | −0.2341 | 0.4009 | −0.58 | 0.559 |
| | lab85 | −0.3676 | 0.1388 | −2.65 | 0.008 |
| | lab89 | 0.1425 | 0.4590 | 0.31 | 0.756 |
| | constant | −0.7005 | 0.7949 | −0.88 | 0.378 |
| Selection | dif | −0.07809 | 0.04656 | −1.68 | 0.093 |
| | age | −0.09474 | 0.02815 | −3.37 | 0.001 |
| | budget | 1.75E−06 | 4.10E−07 | 4.27 | 0.000 |
| | lab83 | −0.6585 | 0.2573 | −2.56 | 0.010 |
| | lab85 | −0.2012 | 0.1892 | −1.06 | 0.288 |
| | lab89 | −0.8691 | 0.3413 | −2.55 | 0.011 |
| | constant | −0.4024 | 0.2795 | −1.44 | 0.150 |
| | athrho | −12.9267 | 313.9783 | −0.04 | 0.967 |
| | $\rho$ | −1 | 7.43E−09 | | |

Number of observations = 316     Censored observations = 273
Uncensored observations = 43     Log likelihood = −131.0742
Wald $\chi^2(4)$ = 11.71     Prob > $\chi^2$ = 0.0196
LR test of independent equations ($\rho$ = 0): $\chi^2(1)$ = 4.08; Prob > $\chi^2$ = 0.0434

Notes
The larger model analogous to the other estimated models (including age in the performance equation) would not converge. Examining just the performance equation suggests that age is not an important factor here, but in any case with the sample remaining for estimation, we cannot jointly estimate the larger model.

Note that there are just 316 projects for the probit model with selection, because from the original 510 projects, the 89 projects from lab81, the 68 projects from lab84, and the 18 projects from lab86 are dropped because they predict perfectly that the project is ahead of schedule, and the 19 projects from lab87 are dropped because there were no respondents to the hypothetical questions from lab87: 510 − 89 − 68 − 18 − 19 = 316.

So, in Table 4.26, just the budget enters the substantive equation (although age is included in the selection equation as usual). The key finding, if one trusted the model's results, would be that the probability of being ahead of schedule because of the ATP funding is essentially 1.0 for all laboratories, rather than being as low as two-thirds for some of the laboratories as indicated in the responses shown in Table 4.25. The variance in the percentages of projects reporting that they are ahead would result because of the response bias – again, if we decide to trust the model here. Although the correlation in the disturbances of the response and the substantive model are strongly negative (estimated to be −1), the standard error for the estimated correlation is very large. The test for the independence of the

*Table 4.27* Predicted probability of being ahead of the hypothetical project

| Laboratory | Number of projects | Probability (%) |
|---|---|---|
| Electronics and Electrical Engineering (81) | 89 | 100 |
| Manufacturing Engineering (82) | 72 | 97 |
| Chemical Science and Technology (83) | 85 | 95 |
| Physics (84) | 68 | 100 |
| Material Science and Engineering (85) | 115 | 95 |
| Building and Fire Research (86) | 18 | 100 |
| Computer Systems (87) | 19 | — |
| Information Technology (89) | 44 | 98 |

equations, however, shows that they are unlikely to be independent. In any case, whether one believes the predictions of the model, or simply takes the lower estimates reported in Table 4.25, ATP intramural projects are quite likely to be ahead of schedule because of the ATP funding.

To summarize the findings from the model: the probabilities for being ahead for projects in lab81, lab84, and lab86 are estimated to be 1.0 given the perfect prediction for those laboratories. Laboratory 87 had no respondents to the hypothetical questions and hence we omit it from the estimated probabilities. Using the probit model with control for response to estimate the probability of being ahead for each project and then averaging the probabilities for projects in each laboratory, we find the probabilities for the remaining laboratories as shown in Table 4.27. Accepting with caution the model as discussed in the preceding paragraph, then response bias is essentially the reason that laboratories 82, 83, 85, and 89 report, as seen in Table 4.25, lower probability of being ahead. Essentially all the laboratories show for their ATP funded projects a probability of being ahead that is very close to 1.0. The strong negative correlation in the disturbances in the response probit and the probit for being ahead of schedule resulted in the lower reported percentages for being ahead in laboratories 82, 83, 85, and 89.

Table 4.25 shows as well the average number of months ahead of schedule for the projects in each lab reporting being ahead. The data for months ahead were examined with the Heckman model of regression with selection.[11] The selection model is reported in Table 4.28, and it is used to predict the number of months ahead of schedule for the average project in each laboratory (except lab87, which provided no responses for this question), and the results are shown in Table 4.29. The errors for the response model and the model for the months ahead of schedule are negatively

*Table 4.28* Model for the number of months ahead of schedule

| Model | Variable | Coefficient | Standard error | z | P > \|z\| |
|---|---|---|---|---|---|
| Q10b | ln budget | 3.8107 | 1.0308 | 3.70 | 0.000 |
| | lab82 | −1.5438 | 3.2050 | −0.48 | 0.630 |
| | lab83 | −4.5878 | 3.4157 | −1.34 | 0.179 |
| | lab84 | −4.5726 | 3.1102 | −1.47 | 0.142 |
| | lab85 | −4.6500 | 2.8586 | −1.63 | 0.104 |
| | lab86 | −1.2125 | 6.9311 | −0.17 | 0.861 |
| | lab89 | −2.8269 | 4.4121 | −0.64 | 0.522 |
| | constant | −27.1367 | 16.2870 | −1.67 | 0.096 |
| Selection | dif | 0.01267 | 0.05531 | 0.23 | 0.819 |
| | age | −0.06494 | 0.03287 | −1.98 | 0.048 |
| | budget | 1.28E−06 | 3.66E−07 | 3.49 | 0.000 |
| | lab82 | 0.4909 | 0.2630 | 1.87 | 0.062 |
| | lab83 | −0.09354 | 0.2879 | −0.32 | 0.745 |
| | lab84 | 0.5878 | 0.2586 | 2.27 | 0.023 |
| | lab85 | 0.2964 | 0.2414 | 1.23 | 0.219 |
| | lab86 | −0.2721 | 0.5322 | −0.51 | 0.609 |
| | lab89 | −0.2575 | 0.3558 | −0.72 | 0.469 |
| | constant | −1.2033 | 0.2995 | −4.02 | 0.000 |
| | athrho | −0.4780 | 0.5253 | −0.91 | 0.363 |
| | ln $\sigma$ | 1.9320 | 0.1960 | 9.86 | 0.000 |
| | $\rho$ | −0.4447 | 0.4214 | | |
| | $\sigma$ | 6.9033 | 1.3529 | | |
| | $\lambda$ | −3.0696 | 3.4594 | | |

Number of observations = 491　　　　　Censored observations = 424
Uncensored observations = 67　　　　　Log likelihood = −399.9063
Wald $\chi^2(7)$ = 19.90　　　　　　　　Prob > $\chi^2$ = 0.0058
LR test of independent equations ($\rho$ = 0): $\chi^2(1)$ = 0.57; Prob > $\chi^2$ = 0.4491

Note
The larger model, with age in the substantive equation for the number of months ahead, would not converge for this sample.

correlated; hence, the predicted number of months is greater than was suggested by the reported number in Table 4.25. However, we cannot reject the null hypothesis of the independence of the errors. As usual, the response model shows that PIs for older projects were less likely to respond while those having projects with larger budgets were more likely to respond, but there is not a clear statistically significant response effect in the number of months ahead that are reported. For that reason, the most reliable information is probably simply the data for average months ahead as reported in Table 4.25.

*Table 4.29* The predicted number of months ahead of schedule

| Laboratory | Number of projects | Average months |
|---|---|---|
| Electronics and Electrical Engineering (81) | 89 | 16 |
| Manufacturing Engineering (82) | 72 | 15 |
| Chemical Science and Technology (83) | 85 | 12 |
| Physics (84) | 68 | 12 |
| Material Science and Engineering (85) | 115 | 12 |
| Building and Fire Research (86) | 18 | 15 |
| Computer Systems (87) | 19 | — |
| Information Technology (89) | 44 | 14 |
| All | 510 − 19 = 491 | 14 |

*Table 4.30* Scope of ATP intramural project compared to the similar hypothetical project

| Laboratory | Number of projects | Broader in scope (%) |
|---|---|---|
| Electronics and Electrical Engineering (81) | 8 | 63 |
| Manufacturing Engineering (82) | 15 | 53 |
| Chemical Science and Technology (83) | 7 | 86 |
| Physics (84) | 17 | 53 |
| Material Science and Engineering (85) | 18 | 28 |
| Building and Fire Research (86) | 1 | 0 |
| Computer Systems (87) | 0 | — |
| Information Technology (89) | 3 | 33 |
| All | 69 | 49 |

Notes
For those who would have undertaken a project with similar goals and milestones absent ATP intramural funding: how does this ATP intramural project compare to the project with similar goals and milestones that you would have undertaken without ATP funding? Is it broader in scope? Yes = 1, No = 0.

Table 4.30 shows that, on average ($n = 69$), 49 percent of the ATP intramural projects reported that they were broader in scope than the hypothetical projects. Again there is a negative correlation in the errors for the response probit and the probit for broader scope, resulting in greater response corrected predictions for the probability of an ATP supported project having broader scope. The correlation, while perfectly negative, is not significant, although the response and the scope equations do not appear to be independent. Table 4.31 shows the probit model for broader scope with control for response. The observations for lab86

*Table 4.31* Probit model for broader scope as compared with the hypothetical project and with control for response

| Model | Variable | Coefficient | Standard error | z | P > |z| |
|---|---|---|---|---|---|
| Q10c | lab82 | −0.6508 | 0.3363 | −1.94 | 0.053 |
| | lab83 | 0.3218 | 0.4652 | 0.69 | 0.489 |
| | lab84 | −0.5903 | 0.3179 | −1.86 | 0.063 |
| | lab85 | −0.6952 | 0.2648 | −2.63 | 0.009 |
| | lab89 | −0.06919 | 0.4111 | −0.17 | 0.866 |
| | constant | 1.8552 | 0.2535 | 7.32 | 0.000 |
| Selection | age | −0.05229 | 0.01306 | −4.00 | 0.000 |
| | budget | 1.11E−06 | 2.73E−07 | 4.09 | 0.000 |
| | lab82 | 0.4616 | 0.2557 | 1.81 | 0.071 |
| | lab83 | −0.1161 | 0.2777 | −0.42 | 0.676 |
| | lab84 | 0.6990 | 0.2503 | 2.79 | 0.005 |
| | lab85 | 0.2686 | 0.2047 | 1.31 | 0.190 |
| | lab89 | −0.2572 | 0.3436 | −0.75 | 0.454 |
| | constant | −1.1925 | 0.1939 | −6.15 | 0.000 |
| | athrho | −10.4403 | 130.7562 | −0.08 | 0.936 |
| | $\rho$ | −1 | 4.47E−07 | | |

Number of observations = 473      Censored observations = 405
Uncensored observations = 68      Log likelihood = −221.2145
Wald $\chi^2(5) = 15.43$      Prob $> \chi^2 = 0.0087$
LR test of independent equations ($\rho = 0$): $\chi^2(1) = 3.90$; Prob $> \chi^2 = 0.0482$

Notes
The 18 observations for lab86 were dropped because they are predicted perfectly, and the observations for lab87 were dropped because we have no respondents from lab87 for the hypothetical questions. Thus the sample size is 510 − 18 − 19 = 473. For this sample, the larger model with age and budget in the substantive model and with age, budget, and dif in the selection model, could not be estimated (the estimation would not converge).

are dropped because they predict perfectly and the observations for lab87 are dropped because we have no respondents from lab87 for the hypothetical questions. For completeness, Table 4.32 shows the probabilities for broader scope for the average project as predicted by the model, although given its uncertainties, the respondents' reports as summarized in Table 4.30 are probably the best indication about scope relative to hypothetical projects.

Table 4.33 shows that, on average ($n = 66$), 58 percent of the ATP intramural projects are more technically challenging than the hypothetical projects. The maximum likelihood probit model (with control for selection) for greater technical challenge shows that the correlation coefficient $\rho$ between the errors in the probit model for technical challenge and the probit model

*Table 4.32* The predicted probabilities of broader scope as compared with the hypothetical project

| Laboratory | Number of projects | Probability (%) |
|---|---|---|
| Electronics and Electrical Engineering (81) | 89 | 100 |
| Manufacturing Engineering (82) | 72 | 90 |
| Chemical Science and Technology (83) | 85 | 99 |
| Physics (84) | 68 | 90 |
| Material Science and Engineering (85) | 115 | 88 |
| Building and Fire Research (86) | 18 | 100* |
| Computer Systems (87) | 19 | — |
| Information Technology (89) | 44 | 96 |

Note
* This prediction is based on a single observation and should therefore be discounted accordingly.

*Table 4.33* Technical challenge of ATP intramural project compared to the similar hypothetical project

| Laboratory | Number of projects | More technically challenging (%) |
|---|---|---|
| Electronics and Electrical Engineering (81) | 8 | 75 |
| Manufacturing Engineering (82) | 15 | 73 |
| Chemical Science and Technology (83) | 6 | 67 |
| Physics (84) | 15 | 33 |
| Material Science and Engineering (85) | 18 | 50 |
| Building and Fire Research (86) | 1 | 100 |
| Computer Systems (87) | 0 | — |
| Information Technology (89) | 3 | 67 |
| All | 66 | 58 |

Notes
For those who would have undertaken a project with similar goals and milestones absent ATP intramural funding: how does this ATP intramural project compare to the project with similar goals and milestones that you would have undertaken without ATP funding? Is it more technically challenging? Yes = 1, No = 0.

for response is not significantly different from zero. Further, the response model and the model of technical challenge are clearly independent of one another. As with the response to the other questions, response was more likely for projects with larger budgets, and response was less likely for the older projects. However, there is no response bias in the answers to this question, and the best model is simply the model shown in Table 4.34 that

*Table 4.34* Probit model for the ATP project being more technically challenging than the hypothetical project

| Variable | Coefficient | Standard error | $z$ | $P > |z|$ |
|---|---|---|---|---|
| age | −0.1449 | 0.07077 | −2.05 | 0.041 |
| lab82 | 0.07224 | 0.6040 | 0.12 | 0.905 |
| lab83 | −0.3276 | 0.7203 | −0.45 | 0.649 |
| lab84 | −0.9121 | 0.6026 | −1.51 | 0.130 |
| lab85 | −0.6645 | 0.5706 | −1.16 | 0.244 |
| lab89 | −0.3765 | 0.8852 | −0.43 | 0.671 |
| constant | 1.3902 | 0.5989 | 2.32 | 0.020 |

Number of observations = 65      LR $\chi^2(6) = 11.31$
Prob $> \chi^2 = 0.0794$      Log likelihood $= -38.7762$
Pseudo $R^2 = 0.1272$

Note
The one observation for lab86 is dropped because it is perfectly predicted, and there are no observations from lab87 for this question.

*Table 4.35* The predicted probability that a project will be more technically challenging than the hypothetical project

| Laboratory | Number of projects | Probability (%) |
|---|---|---|
| Electronics and Electrical Engineering (81) | 89 | 68 |
| Manufacturing Engineering (82) | 72 | 69 |
| Chemical Science and Technology (83) | 85 | 59 |
| Physics (84) | 68 | 36 |
| Material Science and Engineering (85) | 115 | 48 |
| Building and Fire Research (86) | 18 | 100* |
| Computer Systems (87) | 19 | — |
| Information Technology (89) | 44 | 67 |

Note
* This prediction is based on a single observation and should therefore be discounted accordingly.

uses the laboratory effects and then just the significant variables among the remaining explanatory variables. Table 4.35 shows the predicted probabilities across the laboratories.

From this point, because the sample sizes for the various responses to the hypothetical questions become small, we do not attempt to estimate the maximum likelihood models with control for the sample selection by response to the survey. However, we have been able to do enough estimation with control for sample selection to illustrate how selection into the sample can influence reported statistics. In some cases there is no response effect, but in other cases there is an important effect. We have seen that the control for the correlation in the errors in the response models and the models of substantive interest (regarding the performance of the projects) can at times imply that the average performance of the ATP intramural projects responding to the survey exceeds the performance for the nonresponding projects, although that was not uniformly the case. Certainly the ATP-funded projects have been productive, and the reported observations about the hypothetical questions described in the remainder of this appendix continue to support the conclusion that the ATP-funded projects are very productive.

Table 4.36, complementing Table 4.25, shows that on average ($n = 67$), the expected durations of 55 percent of the ATP intramural projects are shorter than for the hypothetical projects.

Tables 4.37 though 4.40 relate to various technical outputs from the ATP intramural project compared to the hypothetical project. Note particularly that many PIs left some or all of these questions blank and thus the number of

*Table 4.36* Expected duration of ATP intramural project compared to the similar hypothetical project

| Laboratory | Number of projects | Longer (%) | Same (%) | Shorter (%) |
|---|---|---|---|---|
| Electronics and Electrical Engineering (81) | 8 | 50 | 0 | 50 |
| Manufacturing Engineering (82) | 14 | 14 | 36 | 50 |
| Chemical Science and Technology (83) | 7 | 14 | 57 | 29 |
| Physics (84) | 16 | 0 | 19 | 81 |
| Material Science and Engineering (85) | 18 | 17 | 28 | 56 |
| Building and Fire Research (86) | 1 | 0 | 100 | 0 |
| Computer Systems (87) | 0 | — | — | — |
| Information Technology (89) | 3 | 33 | 33 | 33 |
| All | 67 | 16 | 28 | 55 |

Notes
For those who would have undertaken a project with similar goals and milestones absent ATP intramural funding: how does this ATP intramural project compare to the project with similar goals and milestones that you would have undertaken without ATP funding? Is the expected duration/time to completion longer/the same/shorter?

*Table 4.37* Expected technical papers from the ATP intramural project compared to the similar hypothetical project

| Laboratory | Number of projects | More (%) | Less (%) | Different (%) | Same (%) |
|---|---|---|---|---|---|
| Electronics and Electrical Engineering (81) | 8 | 100 | 0 | 0 | 0 |
| Manufacturing Engineering (82) | 12 | 75 | 0 | 17 | 8 |
| Chemical Science and Technology (83) | 7 | 71 | 14 | 0 | 14 |
| Physics (84) | 17 | 71 | 0 | 18 | 12 |
| Material Science and Engineering (85) | 15 | 53 | 13 | 20 | 13 |
| Building and Fire Research (86) | 1 | 100 | 0 | 0 | 0 |
| Computer Systems (87) | 0 | — | — | — | — |
| Information Technology (89) | 2 | 50 | 0 | 0 | 50 |
| All | 62 | 71 | 5 | 13 | 12 |

Notes
For those who would have undertaken a project with similar goals and milestones absent ATP intramural funding: how does this ATP intramural project compare to the project with similar goals and milestones that you would have undertaken without ATP funding? Do you think that ATP funding led to more/less/different/same number of technical papers compared to the project that you would have undertaken without ATP funding?

*Table 4.38* Expected new measurement technology from the ATP intramural project compared to the similar hypothetical project

| Laboratory | Number of projects | More (%) | Less (%) | Different (%) | Same (%) |
|---|---|---|---|---|---|
| Electronics and Electrical Engineering (81) | 7 | 100 | 0 | 0 | 0 |
| Manufacturing Engineering (82) | 9 | 56 | 0 | 11 | 33 |
| Chemical Science and Technology (83) | 6 | 17 | 33 | 17 | 33 |
| Physics (84) | 15 | 80 | 0 | 0 | 20 |
| Material Science and Engineering (85) | 14 | 57 | 7 | 29 | 7 |
| Building and Fire Research (86) | 1 | 100 | 0 | 0 | 0 |
| Computer Systems (87) | 0 | — | — | — | — |
| Information Technology (89) | 1 | 0 | 0 | 0 | 100 |
| All | 53 | 64 | 6 | 11 | 19 |

Notes
For those who would have undertaken a project with similar goals and milestones absent ATP intramural funding: how does this ATP intramural project compare to the project with similar goals and milestones that you would have undertaken without ATP funding? Do you think that ATP funding led to more/less/different/same new measurement technology compared to the project that you would have undertaken without ATP funding?

*Table 4.39* Expected new standards from the ATP intramural project compared to the similar hypothetical project

| Laboratory | Number of projects | More (%) | Less (%) | Different (%) | Same (%) |
|---|---|---|---|---|---|
| Electronics and Electrical Engineering (81) | 5 | 20 | 0 | 0 | 80 |
| Manufacturing Engineering (82) | 7 | 71 | 0 | 0 | 29 |
| Chemical Science and Technology (83) | 5 | 0 | 20 | 0 | 80 |
| Physics (84) | 9 | 67 | 0 | 0 | 33 |
| Material Science and Engineering (85) | 4 | 50 | 0 | 0 | 50 |
| Building and Fire Research (86) | 0 | — | — | — | — |
| Computer Systems (87) | 0 | — | — | — | — |
| Information Technology (89) | 2 | 50 | 0 | 0 | 50 |
| All | 32 | 47 | 3 | 0 | 50 |

Notes
For those who would have undertaken a project with similar goals and milestones absent ATP intramural funding: how does this ATP intramural project compare to the project with similar goals and milestones that you would have undertaken without ATP funding? Do you think that ATP funding led to more/less/different/same new standards compared to the project that you would have undertaken without ATP funding?

*Table 4.40* Expected new databases from the ATP intramural project compared to the similar hypothetical project

| Laboratory | Number of projects | More (%) | Less (%) | Different (%) | Same (%) |
|---|---|---|---|---|---|
| Electronics and Electrical Engineering (81) | 4 | 0 | 0 | 0 | 100 |
| Manufacturing Engineering (82) | 6 | 67 | 0 | 0 | 33 |
| Chemical Science and Technology (83) | 5 | 40 | 20 | 0 | 40 |
| Physics (84) | 5 | 0 | 0 | 0 | 100 |
| Material Science and Engineering (85) | 4 | 50 | 0 | 0 | 50 |
| Building and Fire Research (86) | 1 | 100 | 0 | 0 | 0 |
| Computer Systems (87) | 0 | — | — | — | — |
| Information Technology (89) | 1 | 0 | 0 | 0 | 100 |
| All | 26 | 35 | 4 | 0 | 62 |

Notes
For those who would have undertaken a project with similar goals and milestones absent ATP intramural funding: how does this ATP intramural project compare to the project with similar goals and milestones that you would have undertaken without ATP funding? Do you think that ATP funding led to more/less/different/same new databases compared to the project that you would have undertaken without ATP funding?

reporting projects is less than for previous questions. While these small laboratory samples create interpretative problems, the overall percentage responses show that ATP intramural projects, in comparison to the hypothetical projects with similar goals and milestones that would have been undertaken without ATP funding, are expected to lead to more technical papers, more new measurement technology, more or at least the same number of new standards, and the same number of new databases.

Of the 62 responding ATP intramural projects in Table 4.37, 71 percent are expected to lead to more technical papers than from the hypothetical projects. Of the 53 responding ATP intramural projects in Table 4.38, 64 percent are expected to lead to more new measurement technology. In Table 4.39, only 3 percent of the ATP intramural projects are expected to lead to fewer new standards, meaning that 97 percent are expected to lead to more or at least the same number of new standards. And, as shown in Table 4.40, only 4 percent of the 26 responding ATP intramural projects expected fewer new databases in comparison to the hypothetical projects, meaning that 96 percent are expected to lead to more or at least the same number of new databases. PIs were similarly asked about patents; the 17 responding projects show that they would be about the same, which is close to zero as noted above.

As shown in Table 4.22, PIs responded that for 70 (46 percent) of the 151 projects they would have undertaken a project with similar goals and

*Table 4.41* Probability of undertaking a broadly related research project absent ATP intramural funding

| Laboratory | Number of projects | Probability (%) |
|---|---|---|
| Electronics and Electrical Engineering (81) | 12 | 33 |
| Manufacturing Engineering (82) | 15 | 33 |
| Chemical Science and Technology (83) | 9 | 22 |
| Physics (84) | 6 | 100 |
| Material Science and Engineering (85) | 23 | 57 |
| Building and Fire Research (86) | 2 | 50 |
| Computer Systems (87) | 3 | 0 |
| Information Technology (89) | 11 | 9 |
| All | 81 | 40 |

Notes
If you would not have undertaken a research project with similar goals and milestones in the absence of ATP intramural funding, would you alternatively have undertaken a project in the same broadly defined research area as your ATP intramural project? Yes = 1, No = 0. When making this comparison, please consider a hypothetical project with an amount of funding comparable to your ATP intramural project.

*Table 4.42* Scope of ATP intramural project compared to the hypothetical broadly defined project

| Laboratory | Number of projects | Broader in scope (%) |
|---|---|---|
| All | 31 | 52 |

Notes
For those who would not have undertaken a project with similar goals and milestones absent ATP intramural funding but would have undertaken a project in the same broadly defined research area: how does this ATP intramural project compare to the project in the same broadly defined area that you would have undertaken without ATP funding? Is it broader in scope? Yes = 1, No = 0.

*Table 4.43* Technical challenge of ATP intramural project compared to the broadly defined hypothetical project

| Laboratory | Number of projects | More technically challenging (%) |
|---|---|---|
| All | 31 | 48 |

Notes
For those who would not have undertaken a project with similar goals and milestones absent ATP intramural funding but would have undertaken a project in the same broadly defined research area: how does this ATP intramural project compare to the project in the same broadly defined area that you would have undertaken without ATP funding? Is it more technically challenging? Yes = 1, No = 0.

*Table 4.44* Expected duration of ATP intramural project compared to the broadly defined hypothetical project

| Laboratory | Number of projects | Longer (%) | Same (%) | Shorter (%) |
|---|---|---|---|---|
| All | 31 | 45 | 16 | 39 |

Notes
For those who would not have undertaken a project with similar goals and milestones absent ATP intramural funding but would have undertaken a project in the same broadly defined research area: how does this ATP intramural project compare to the project in the same broadly defined area that you would have undertaken without ATP funding? Is the expected duration/time to completion longer/the same/shorter?

milestones in the absence of funding for their ATP intramural project. For those 81 projects that would not have done so, PIs were asked if they would have alternatively undertaken a project in the same broadly defined research area. As shown in Table 4.41, 39.57 percent of the projects would have been undertaken in the same broadly defined research area. Because the

*Table 4.45* Expected technical papers from the ATP intramural project compared to the broadly defined hypothetical project

| Laboratory | Number of projects | More (%) | Less (%) | Different (%) | Same (%) |
|---|---|---|---|---|---|
| All | 27 | 44 | 30 | 19 | 7 |

Notes
For those who would not have undertaken a project with similar goals and milestones absent ATP intramural funding but would have undertaken a project in the same broadly defined research area: how does this ATP intramural project compare to the project in the same broadly defined area that you would have undertaken without ATP funding? Do you think that ATP funding led to more/less/different/same number of technical papers compared to the project that you would have undertaken without ATP funding?

*Table 4.46* Expected new measurement technology from the ATP intramural project compared to the broadly defined hypothetical project

| Laboratory | Number of projects | More (%) | Less (%) | Different (%) | Same (%) |
|---|---|---|---|---|---|
| All | 21 | 57 | 14 | 19 | 10 |

Notes
For those who would not have undertaken a project with similar goals and milestones absent ATP intramural funding but would have undertaken a project in the same broadly defined research area: how does this ATP intramural project compare to the project in the same broadly defined area that you would have undertaken without ATP funding? Do you think that ATP funding led to more/less/different/same new measurement technology compared to the project that you would have undertaken without ATP funding?

*Table 4.47* Expected new standards from the ATP intramural project compared to the broadly defined hypothetical project

| Laboratory | Number of projects | More (%) | Less (%) | Different (%) | Same (%) |
|---|---|---|---|---|---|
| All | 17 | 53 | 12 | 6 | 29 |

Notes
For those who would not have undertaken a project with similar goals and milestones absent ATP intramural funding but would have undertaken a project in the same broadly defined research area: how does this ATP intramural project compare to the project in the same broadly defined area that you would have undertaken without ATP funding? Do you think that ATP funding led to more/less/different/same new standards compared to the project that you would have undertaken without ATP funding?

*Table 4.48* Expected new databases from the ATP intramural project compared to the broadly defined hypothetical project

| Laboratory | Number of projects | More (%) | Less (%) | Different (%) | Same (%) |
|---|---|---|---|---|---|
| All | 16 | 19 | 25 | 6 | 50 |

Notes

For those who would not have undertaken a project with similar goals and milestones absent ATP intramural funding but would have undertaken a project in the same broadly defined research area: how does this ATP intramural project compare to the project in the same broadly defined area that you would have undertaken without ATP funding? Do you think that ATP funding led to more/less/different/same new databases compared to the project that you would have undertaken without ATP funding?

total number of projects that fall within this category is small, only all laboratory means are reported in Tables 4.42–4.48. Specifically, for those projects that would not have been undertaken with similar goals and milestones but would alternatively have been undertaken in the same broadly defined research area: 51.61 percent are expected to be broader in scope (see Table 4.42); 48 percent are expected to be more technically challenging (see Table 4.43); 39 percent are expected to be of shorter duration (see Table 4.44); 44 percent are expected to generate more technical papers (see Table 4.45); 57 percent are expected to generate more new measurement technology (see Table 4.46); 53 percent are expected to generate more standards (see Table 4.47); and 69 percent are expected to generate more or at least the same number of new databases (see Table 4.48).

# 5    Case study selection and methodology

Four detailed case studies were conducted as part of our evaluation of ATP's intramural research program.

## Selection process

During an initial December 2000 meeting with the directors of the three technical offices within ATP – chemistry and life sciences (CLS), electronics and photonics technology (EPT), and information technology (IT) – each director was asked to identify four or five intramural research projects for possible case study.[1]

Two criteria were offered to the directors to guide their initial selection process:

- the ATP intramural project must have documentable technical outputs and industrial applications;
- the intramural project's PI must currently be employed at NIST.

During a second meeting with the directors and selected intramural project mangers (PMs) in February 2001, 16 candidate projects were recommended. As shown in Table 5.1, four projects were suggested from CLS, seven from EPT, and five from IT. After this second meeting, in person and/or telephone interviews were held with the identified PMs.

Twelve of sixteen PIs associated with the projects listed in Table 5.1 were interviewed face-to-face at NIST-Gaithersburg; three PIs were at NIST-Boulder and were interviewed by telephone; the 16th PI is at NIST-Gaithersburg, but he declined to be interviewed or to participate in the study. Based on these interviews, we reduced the population of candidate projects from 16 to 9. This was a subjective reduction, taking into account whether there actually were at that time documentable technical outputs and outcomes with socially valuable industrial applications and taking into account the willingness of the PI to participate in a follow-up case study.[2]

*Table 5.1* Initial candidate intramural research projects for case study

| Technical office | Project title | Funding history |
|---|---|---|
| CLS | *Injectable Composite Bone Grafts: Biocompatability and Comparability* | *FY 1999–2001* |
| CLS | Infrastructure for Development of Selective Membrane Platforms | FY 1998–2000 |
| CLS | Microstructure Characterization by Nondestructive Imaging for Permeability Prediction and Failure Mechanism Evaluation | FY 1998–2000 |
| CLS | Fatigue Resistance of High Performance Polymeric Composite Immersed in Sea Water | FY 1998–2000 |
| EPT | *Wavelength References for Optical Fiber Communications* | *FY 1998–1999* |
| EPT | A Novel Method for Fabricating Critical Dimension Reference Materials with 100 nm Linewidths | FY 1999–2000 |
| EPT | Compound Semiconductor Composition Standards | FY 1998–2000 |
| EPT | *Polymer Composite Dielectrics for Integrated Thin-Film Capacitors* | *FY 1999–2001* |
| EPT | *Optimal Design of NIST Microactuators for Precision Machines (and follow on work under the title Deformable Structure Micro Positioners)* | *FY 1998–2001* |
| EPT | In-Situ Measurement of Temperature for Semiconductor and Thin-Film Processing | FY 1997–1998 |
| EPT | Interconnect, Probe/Test Fixture, and Material Characterization Using Advanced Time Domain Measurements | FY 1999–2001 |
| IT | *NIST WebMetrics Project* | *FY 1998* |
| IT | *Development of Methodology and Function Security Architecture for Construction of ISO/IEC 15408 Security Protection Profiles for Healthcare Information Systems* | *FY 1999–2001* |
| IT | *Fundamental Studies of Dislocation Structures During Deformation* | *FY 1998–2000* |
| IT | *Machine Tool Characterization Monitoring and Control* | *FY 1996–1998* |
| IT | *Internet Commerce for Manufacturing* | *FY 1998–2000* |

Table 5.2 Sub-sample of nine candidate intramural research projects for case study

| Technical office | Project title | PI | PI's laboratory | Project's output |
|---|---|---|---|---|
| CLS | Injectable Composite Bone Grafts: Biocompatability and Comparability | Wang | MSEL | Product |
| EPT | Wavelength References for Optical Fiber Communications | Gilbert | EEEL | Standard Reference Material Test Method |
| EPT | Polymer Composite Dielectrics for Integrated Thin-Film Capacitors | Obrzut | MSEL | |
| IT | Internet Commerce for Manufacturing | Rhodes et al. | ITL, MEL, EEEL | Standard |
| EPT | Optimal Design of NIST Microactuators for Precision Machines (and follow on work under the title Deformable Structure Micro Positioners) | Dagalakis | MEL | Product, Test and Calibration Methods |
| IT | NIST WebMetrics Project | Laskowski | ITL | Tool |
| IT | Development of Methodology and Function Security Architecture for Construction of ISO/IEC 15408 Security Protection Profiles for Healthcare Information Systems | Johnson | ITL | Standard |
| IT | Fundamental Studies of Dislocation Structures During Deformation | Fields | MSEL | Product |
| IT | Machine Tool Characterization Monitoring and Control | Donmez | MEL | Standard |

Notes
MSEL  Material Science and Engineering Laboratory.
EEEL  Electronics and Electrical Engineering Laboratory.
MEL   Manufacturing Engineering Laboratory.
ITL   Information Technology Laboratory.

The nine projects selected for consideration for detailed case studies are noted in italics in Table 5.1 and summarized in more detail in Table 5.2. In April 2002, this group of nine was presented for discussion purposes to ATP along with our recommendations for four detailed case studies. Our recommendations were based in part on having talked with individuals in industry, who had been identified by the PI, about measurable benefits and the likelihood of identifying others with whom we could talk, and in part on having a cross-technical office and a cross-NIST laboratory representation. The justification for our recommendations was discussed among the ATP staff at the meeting before our recommended four projects were chosen as the ones for the more detailed case studies.

The four projects selected for case studies (in italics in Table 5.2) are not necessarily representative of the population of ATP intramural projects, or of projects for which the PI was still at NIST, or of projects with identifiable outputs. Our selection of the four projects was based on the objective and subjective criteria described above, and the evaluation findings from the four case studies in this book should be interpreted in that light. Those selected were believed to be among the more successful (but not necessarily the most successful) projects in addressing the intramural program mission based on the screening process. Generalizations from the four case studies to the population of ATP intramural projects would not typically be appropriate.

## Systematic evaluation methodology

Fundamental to an evaluation of any federal program, for research or otherwise, is that the program is accountable to the public. For research programs, such accountability refers to being able to document and evaluate research performance using metrics that are meaningful to the institutions' stakeholders – the public, including the taxpayers.[3] Metrics developed for assessing returns to private investment have been adapted to public investments using case study techniques that emphasize analysis of public benefits to research users and taxpayers.

With any performance evaluation, it is generally assumed that the government has an economically justifiable role in supporting innovation because of market failures stemming from, among other things, the private sector's inability to appropriate returns to investments, the public-good nature of the research focus, or the riskiness of those investments.[4] Ignoring such an assumption may imply that any evaluation of a public research program is wanting in the sense that the program has not been scrutinized initially on first principles as to why it is even undertaking research.

Griliches (1958) and Mansfield *et al.* (1977) pioneered the application of fundamental economic insight to the development of measurements of private and social rates of return to innovative investments. Streams of investment costs generate streams of economic benefits over time. Once identified and measured, these streams of costs and benefits are used to calculate such performance metrics as social rates of return and benefit-to-cost ratios.

For example, for a process innovation adopted in a competitive market, using the traditional framework, the publicly funded innovation being evaluated is thought to lower the cost of producing a product to be sold in a competitive market. As the innovation lowers the unit cost of production, consumers will actually pay less for the product than they paid before the innovation and less than they would have been willing to pay – a gain in consumer surplus. The social benefits from the innovation include the total savings that all consumers and producers receive as a result of producers having adopted the cost-reducing innovation. Depending on the extent to which reduced costs are reflected in the price charged to consumers, social benefits are shared by producers who adopt the innovation and consumers of their products. Thus, the evaluation question that can be answered from this traditional approach is: Given the investment costs and the social benefits, what is the social rate of return to the innovation?

The traditional evaluation method pioneered by Griliches and Mansfield is used in the four case studies.[5] To implement that method, two general data series are needed. One data series is related to investment costs, and in the case of this study the relevant investment costs are those associated with the ATP intramural project.[6] The other data series is related to the benefits realized by society, net of society's costs to use the innovation (i.e. pull costs). Society includes both private sector companies and consumers. ATP's investment costs are known. Benefit data have to be collected, and these data can be of two types. Benefit data can be retrospective in nature, meaning that the company or consumer who has benefited from the ATP project has already realized benefits; or benefit data can be prospective in nature, meaning that the company or consumer who will benefit in the future from the ATP project can estimate when and to what degree benefits will be realized.[7] Both types of benefit data were collected in this study.

## Social rate of return metrics

Using the time series for costs and benefits measured in constant dollars, the internal rate of return (IRR), the benefit-to-cost ratio, and the net present value (NPV) for the project are calculated in each of the four case studies using the year when each project began as the base year. In addition to those three customary metrics, the NPV referenced to year 2002 was also computed for each case study for comparative purposes.

The metrics are calculated from the time series of costs and benefits in year 2000 dollars. Costs and benefits were converted to constant dollars to allow all dollar figures to be directly comparable. All dollar figures have been converted to year 2000 dollars using the chain-type price index for gross domestic product provided in the *Economic Report of the President*.[8] Year 2000 was chosen because, at the time that the case studies were conducted, that was the most recent year for which complete annual data were available.

### *Internal rate of return*[9]

The IRR is the value of the discount rate, $i$, that equates the NPV of the stream of net benefits associated with a research project to zero.[10] The time series runs from the beginning of the research project, $t = 0$, to a terminal point, $t = n$.

Mathematically,

$$\text{NPV} = [(B_0 - C_0) / (1 + i)^0] + \cdots + [(B_n - C_n) / (1 + i)^n] = 0, \tag{1}$$

where $(B_t - C_t)$ represents the net benefits associated with the project in year $t$, and $n$ represents the number of time periods – years in the case studies evaluated in this book – being considered in the evaluation.

For unique solutions for $i$, from equation (1), the IRR can be compared to a value, $r$, that represents the opportunity cost of funds invested by the technology-based public institution.[11] Thus, if the opportunity cost of funds is less than the internal rate of return, the project was worthwhile from an *ex post* social perspective.

### *Benefit-to-cost ratio*

The ratio of benefits-to-costs (*B/C*) is the ratio of the present value of all measured benefits to the present value of all measured costs. Both benefits and costs are referenced to the initial time period, $t = 0$, when the project began as:

$$\frac{B}{C} = \frac{\sum_{t=0 \text{ to } t=n} B_t / (1+r)^t}{\sum_{t=0 \text{ to } t=n} C_t / (1+r)^t} \tag{2}$$

A benefit-to-cost ratio of 1 is said to indicate a project that breaks even. Any project with $B/C > 1$ is a relatively successful project as defined in terms of benefits exceeding costs.

Fundamental to implementing the ratio of benefits-to-costs is a value for the discount rate, $r$. While the discount rate representing the opportunity cost for public funds could differ across a portfolio of public investments, the calculated metrics in this book follow the guidelines set forth by the Office of Management and Budget in Circular A-94 (1992), which states that: "Constant-dollar benefit-cost analyses of proposed investments and regulations should report net present value and other outcomes determined using a real discount rate of 7 percent."

*Net present value*

The information developed to determine the benefit-to-cost ratio can be used to determine NPV as:

$$\text{NPV}_{\text{initial year}} = B - C, \tag{3}$$

where, as in the calculation of $B/C$, $B$ refers to the present value of all measured benefits and $C$ refers to the present value of all measured costs and where present value refers to the initial year or time period in which the project began, $t = 0$ in terms of the $B/C$ formula in equation (2). Note that NPV allows, in principle, one means of ranking several projects *ex post*, providing investment sizes are similar.

To compare the net present values across the four case studies with different starting dates, the net present value for each is brought forward to year 2002. The $\text{NPV}_{\text{initial year}}$ is brought forward under the assumption that the NPV for the project was invested at the 7 percent real rate of return that is recommended by the Office of Management and Budget as the opportunity cost of government funds. $\text{NPV}_{2002}$ is then a project's NPV multiplied by 1.07 raised to the power of 2002 minus the year that the project was initiated as:

$$\text{NPV}_{2002} = \text{NPV} \times (1.07)^{2002 \, - \, \text{initial year}}. \tag{4}$$

# 6    Case study of wavelength references for optical fiber communications

The goal of this project was to develop an improved standard reference material (SRM) for the measurement of the wavelength of light in an optical fiber network.

## Background information and overview of the project

The Optoelectronics Division of the Electronics and Electrical Engineering Laboratory began research on optical communications in the mid-1970s and expanded its research program substantially in the late 1980s. The Optical Fiber and Components Group of the Division began research on SRMs in 1991. The Group's first SRM became available in 1993 with SRM 2520, an optical fiber diameter standard. Since then the Group has produced a number of optoelectronic standards. SRM 2517 was issued in 1997; it was intended for use in calibrating the wavelength scale of wavelength measuring equipment in the spectral region from 1,510 to 1,541 nm.

In 1998, Dr Sarah Gilbert in the Optical Fiber and Components Group began a 2-year ATP intramural project to develop a more accurate version of SRM 2517. Dr Gilbert received $145,000 over 2 years – $70,000 in FY 1998 and $75,000 in FY 1999.

The project produced the new SRM for calibration of wavelengths in the spectral region from 1,510 to 1,540 nm. The references in the 1,500 nm region are important to support wavelength division multiplexed (WDM) optical fiber communications systems. In a WDM system, many channels, each associated with a different wavelength, of communication information are sent down the same fiber. Thus, wavelength division multiplexing in effect increases the bandwidth of the communications system, because any given spectral region will support more channels through which communications information can be sent. A WDM system requires stable wavelengths throughout the components of the system, and equipment must be calibrated to measure those wavelengths. The wavelength references provided by NIST are needed to calibrate the instruments – such as optical spectrum analyzers, tunable lasers, and wavelength meters – that are used to characterize the components of WDM optical fiber communications systems. The wavelength references are also used to monitor the wavelengths of the channels while the system is in use, because if one channel's wavelength were to shift, cross talk could occur between it and a neighboring channel, thus disrupting the accurate flow of communications information through the channels of the system.

The output of Dr Gilbert's ATP-funded NIST research with William Swann was Standard Reference Material 2517a, High Resolution Wavelength Calibration Reference for 1,510–1,540 nm Acetylene ($^{12}C_2H_2$). Quoting NIST's description of the new SRM provides an exact description of the artifact – an "absorption cell" filled with acetylene gas that produces characteristic "absorption lines" in the readouts resulting when lasers project light of various wavelengths through the gas-filled cell. The absorption lines observed can then be used to identify the wavelengths for the laser-emitting device being calibrated.[1] NIST's description of the artifact is as follows:[2]

> Standard Reference Material 2517a is intended for wavelength calibration in the spectral region from 1510 nm to 1540 nm. It is a single-mode optical-fiber-coupled absorption cell containing acetylene ($^{12}C_2H_2$) gas at a pressure of 6.7 kPa (50 Torr). The absorption path length is 5 cm and the absorption lines are about 7 pm wide. The cell is packaged in a small instrument box (approximately 24 cm long $\times$ 12.5 cm wide $\times$ 9 cm high) with two FC/PC fiber connectors for the input and output of a user-supplied light source. Acetylene has more than 50 accurately measured absorption lines in the 1500 nm wavelength region. This SRM can be used for high-resolution applications, such as calibrating a narrowband tunable laser, or lower resolution applications, such as calibrating an optical spectrum analyzer.

The main difference between the new wavelength calibration standard, SRM 2517a, and its predecessor, SRM 2517, is the use of lower pressure in the acetylene cell to produce narrower lines. Because of that difference, SRM 2517a can be used in higher resolution and accuracy applications.

## Implications for industry and society

This ATP intramural project complemented the SRM-related research of the Optical Fiber and Components Group and was a natural extension of previous research related to SRM 2517. While research on SRM 2517a would have occurred in the absence of ATP's support, it would not have progressed as rapidly. According to Dr Gilbert:

> The ATP funding accelerated this project and enabled us to complete the development of a new wavelength calibration SRM about one year faster that we would have without this funding.

Thus, if ATP had not funded the project, the NIST laboratory would have invested a similar amount, but the streams of benefits and costs would have been roughly a year later. In this case study, we evaluate the social rate of return for the project. We do not try to identify the incremental gain from having the project funded by ATP rather than the NIST laboratory that performed the research.

NIST has been selling SRM 2517a at a rate of two to three per month since it was introduced in late 2000.[3]

## Benefit and cost information[4]

Detailed descriptions of the uses of SRM 2517a are provided below, but in overview, NIST's experience suggests that most of the test equipment manufacturers in industry use the SRM units to conduct periodic calibration checks on their equipment. The calibration checks with the SRM are not typically in the production line where various intermediate standards are used for routine calibration checks. Rather, the SRM is used to check those intermediate standards. Some of these test equipment manufacturers make absorption cells – commercial versions of the SRM 2517a artifact described above – to incorporate into their products. In those situations where the absorption cells are purchased, discussions with industry experts reveal that SRM 2517a is used both to check the commercial versions of the absorption cells and for study as a manufacturing guide in the production of the commercial high-volume versions of the cell. Discussions with industry show that the component manufacturers often integrate the SRM 2517a into their production lines to continuously calibrate their equipment. Network systems providers use the SRMs to calibrate their test equipment.

The industry costs and benefits for SRM 2517a are based on estimates – obtained through detailed telephone interviews – from industry respondents that collectively have purchased about 30 percent of the SRM 2517a cells.[5]

Discussions with industry identified several types of benefits and costs associated with SRM 2517a. Benefits fall within five general categories: production-related-engineering experimentation-cost savings, calibration-cost savings, yield, negotiation, and marketing. Costs are the

ATP development costs plus the pull costs associated with using the SRM purchased from NIST.

Separating the SRM 2517a benefits from the benefits of other SRMs in the 25xx family was often difficult for industry respondents.[6] Some use the entire set of SRM 25xx artifacts; those respondents sometimes think of the set of artifacts as an integrated whole, covering different parts of the spectrum of wavelengths to which equipment must be calibrated. Thus, to some extent the benefit estimates below reflect a joint benefit from the set of NIST SRM 25xx artifacts. However, there are also major sources of unmeasured industrial benefits from SRM 2517a. As a result, the benefit estimates used are, on balance, conservative for at least three reasons. First, the estimates are truncated after ten future years, even though some respondents believe that the commercial usefulness of SRM 2517a would extend well beyond that period. Second, and more important, many respondents could not quantify the loss in sales, and therefore profits, that would occur without traceability to NIST of their wavelength calibrations. And third, the benefit estimates reflect only the benefits to the purchasers of the NIST SRM 2517a artifacts; they do not capture the additional benefits to users further down the supply chain. As one respondent whose company manufactures commercial gas cells (based on SRM 2517a) for use in instruments stated: "If there were no SRM 2517a, all along the way through the supply chain the additional calibration expenses (suites of equipment and extra labor costs) would be incurred. Roughly one-half of the optical spectrum analyzers sold to industry incorporate the SRM 2517a technology to calibrate better. There would be extra expense and time at each research site." Given these sources of downward bias, we believe that, on balance, the benefit estimates used to compute the evaluation metrics to characterize the outcomes of SRM 2517a are conservative.

Use of SRM 2517a results in the following savings.

1 *Production related engineering and experimentation cost savings* Users of SRM 2517a regularly conduct what we call production related engineering experimentation.[7] These activities are an important aspect of production. The new, more accurate measurement technology associated with SRM 2517a lowered the cost of these activities and hence represents a cost-savings benefit. Also, experimentation costs for industry have been lowered because of industry's interaction with the NIST scientists that developed the artifact. One industry expert said SRM 2517a reduced his company's investigation costs and added that without it, the company would have invested additional engineering person-years with equipment to maintain production.[8]

*2 Calibration cost savings*   SRM 2517a reduces the costs of calibrating production equipment and products. Examples, based on discussions with respondents in industry, follow.

It is not uncommon to recalibrate production devices for an optical fiber network on a daily basis, or even more frequently. SRM 2517a reduces the cost of each calibration; it permits equipment to be calibrated on the production floor. The alternative would be to purchase tunable lasers, which are not only more costly but also must be set for one frequency at a time, whereas the SRMs provide a fingerprint covering a whole range of the spectrum of wavelengths. In addition, tunable lasers entail additional operating time using well-trained technicians involved in production.

One respondent, whose company manufactures locked lasers and gas cells, observed that the alternative to SRM 2517a for calibration is to invest in a suite of equipment and then take the extra time to get the calibration results. A telecommunications company responded that prior to SRM 2517a it relied on its own internal standards based on one frequency and then extrapolated to other frequencies. The company's expert stated that the SRM 2517a standard, with multiple indicators of various frequencies, is a critically important advance for telecommunications.

*3 Increased production yields*   Production yields have increased because SRM 2517a improved process control and thereby reduced the costs of product failure. Manufacturers of optical fiber network components produce to the customer's specifications and needs. SRM 2517a, as well as other SRMs in the 25xx series, provide useful reference points across a stable wavelength range for the tuning of the components for optical communications systems. As a costly and less accurate alternative, the points of reference could be simulated with cascades of optical filters strung together.

A manufacturer of narrow band optical filters told us: SRM 2517a provides narrow line widths for reference to absolute vacuum wavelengths and this is critical to meeting the performance specification needs of our customers. This artifact gives us an unquestionable reference to absolute wavelengths so that secondary standards can be recalibrated as they drift. Our alternative, over say 30 nm of wavelength range for a particular product, maybe 10 optical filters would be strung together. Whereas the cost of this alternative is not that great, performance tolerances and wavelength stability would be lost. Using the alternative would have resulted in a yield loss of about 30 percent.

*4 Negotiations cost savings*   Negotiations with customers over disputes about the performance attributes of products are reduced because of SRM 2517a and the traceability to the NIST standard that it provides. In the absence of wavelength stability, manufacturers and customers would both have grounds to disagree about performance characteristics. Without SRM 2517a and the traceability that it provides, costly negotiations and testing would occur. One respondent said that without NIST traceability through SRM 2517a, interactions with the customers over performance characteristics would be like dealing with "a wound that would not heal."

5 *Reduced marketing costs*   Marketing costs are reduced because SRM 2517a allows traceability of an important new standard to NIST, and sales are greater than for SRM 2517 because of the confidence inspired by the new standard traceable to NIST.

Paraphrasing a component manufacturer: There are two parts to the sales/marketing impact of SRM 2517a for our company. First, there is a savings in personnel costs because there is less effort needed to convince customers about the quality and reliability of our products. More importantly, there is a positive effect on our reputation and the customers' confidence in our product line because of having NIST standards integrated in the production process. That positive effect translates into extra sales and extra profits. Paraphrasing a manufacturer of wavelength meters: We use SRM 2517a as we manufacture wavelength meters. SRM 2517a is used to check periodically the calibration of test lasers and equipment used for the qualification of our wavemeters. We can claim traceability to NIST. There are cost savings to us in the sales/marketing category.

Quantitative estimates of each of the above categories of benefits were obtained from the five manufacturers with whom we spoke. According to Dr Gilbert, these five companies collectively have purchased about 30 percent of the SRM 2517a cells sold to date. The benefit data in Table 6.1 captures industry-wide benefits. Each datum in Table 6.1 (and in the third column in Table 6.2) is the product of the sum of the dollar values for each respondent multiplied by 3.33 (3.33 = 1/0.30), and all dollar values are converted to year 2000 dollars.

To be conservative, the estimated benefits from SRM 2517a are truncated after ten years. Respondents indicated that the SRM 2517a provided knowledge that would be commercially useful for the foreseeable future. Some respondents emphasized that, as a standard, the knowledge embodied in SRM 2517a would last and be useful virtually forever. However, industry may require even more development of the standards for measuring the wavelength of light as time passes, and the respondents as a group believed that a commercial lifetime of ten years would be a conservative estimate for the period of intense industrial use of SRM 2517a.

The observed variance in benefits (in year 2000 dollars) through time reflects three key things. First, there are different periods of primary incidence for the various cost savings. For example, production-related

Table 6.1 Industry benefits truncated at 10 years (year 2000 dollars)

| Year | Production cost savings ($1,000s) | Calibration cost savings ($1,000s) | Increased production yield ($1,000s) | Decreased negotiation costs ($1,000s) | Decreased marketing costs ($1,000s) |
|---|---|---|---|---|---|
| 1999 | 3,193.9 | | | | |
| 2000 | 3,266.5 | 401.0 | 2,613.3 | 245.0 | 473.7 |
| 2001 | 1,388.3 | 1,832.6 | 10,531.7 | 1,094.3 | 1,894.7 |
| 2002 | 1,682.3 | 353.5 | 2,106.3 | 218.9 | 383.0 |
| 2003 | 1,388.3 | 441.8 | 2,632.9 | 273.6 | 478.8 |
| 2004 | 1,388.3 | 589.7 | 3,514.2 | 365.2 | 639.0 |
| 2005 | 1,388.3 | 735.8 | 4,384.6 | 455.6 | 797.3 |
| 2006 | | 846.8 | 5,046.5 | 524.4 | 917.7 |
| 2007 | | 973.8 | 5,803.2 | 603.0 | 1,055.2 |
| 2008 | | 1,119.9 | 6,673.7 | 693.4 | 1,213.5 |
| 2009 | | 1,287.8 | 7,674.7 | 797.5 | 1,395.6 |

Notes
Production related engineering and experimentation cost savings decrease in 2001 because, although some experimental production uses of the measurement technology were reported after the introduction of the SRM, the most intense realization of such experimental benefits came from the application of the new measurement technology – gained in industry's interaction with NIST through publications, presentations, and ongoing interaction with the researchers – to production problems encountered by industry as it coped with the need for the actual improved SRM and substituted experimentation for it. Publications about the SRM 2517a technology started to appear in 1999. The other categories of industry benefits increase after the introduction of the SRM 2517a because those benefits reflect the actual use of the SRMs once they were available for use.

*Table 6.2* Estimated costs associated with SRM 2517a
(year 2000 dollars)

| Year | ATP funds ($1,000s) | Industry pull cost ($1,000s) |
|------|---------------------|------------------------------|
| 1998 | 72.6 | |
| 1999 | 76.7 | |
| 2000 | | 16.3 |
| 2001 | | 73.5 |

engineering cost savings occur primarily in the early years of the time series and in some cases even before the introduction of SRM 2517a.[9] In contrast, the costs of reduced yields (benefit of increased yields) are avoided throughout the time series after SRM 2517a was introduced and the technology transferred to industry. Second, the introduction of SRM 2517a occurred in late 2000 and partial-year benefits are reported; benefits increase in subsequent years since the SRM is used throughout each year. Third, the variance over time reflects the collapse of optical fiber communications industry sales from record highs in 2000–2001 to low levels in 2002. Projections by industry then reflect an expected recovery of industry sales to the levels experienced in 1999 – levels that in 1999 were between one-third and one-half of their subsequent peaks in 2000–2001 before the bubble burst – by 2004–2005. Thereafter, the projections reflect what knowledgeable industry observers expect to be a 15 percent rate of growth.

The costs associated with the SRM 2517a project are in Table 6.2. The actual costs of the ATP intramural project are shown along with estimates of the pull costs for industry. Respondents were asked to estimate any initial costs, over and above any fees paid to NIST for SRM 2517a, to be able to use (i.e. pull in) the artifact in production. These pull costs are one-time costs.

Table 6.3 aggregates the cost and benefit estimates from Tables 6.1 and 6.2.

## Results of the economic analysis

Table 6.4 summarizes the four evaluation metrics for this case study. Based on one or all of the metrics in Table 6.4, the ATP intramural funded SRM 2517a project was successful from society's economic perspective. The public's extant investment in the Optical Fiber and Components Group enabled a relatively small incremental investment in a refined optoelectronic standard to yield a large social benefit. The internal rate of return is 4,400 percent, the benefit-to-cost ratio is 267 to 1, and the net present value in 2002 in year 2000 dollars is $76 million.

*Table 6.3* Estimated total costs and estimated total
industry benefits associated with SRM
2517a (year 2000 dollars)

| Year | Total costs ($1,000s) | Total industry benefits ($1,000s) |
|------|------------|-------------------|
| 1998 | 72.6 | |
| 1999 | 76.7 | 3,193.9 |
| 2000 | 16.3 | 6,999.5 |
| 2001 | 73.5 | 16,741.6 |
| 2002 | | 4,744.0 |
| 2003 | | 5,215.4 |
| 2004 | | 6,496.4 |
| 2005 | | 7,761.6 |
| 2006 | | 7,335.4 |
| 2007 | | 8,435.2 |
| 2008 | | 9,700.5 |
| 2009 | | 11,155.6 |

*Table 6.4* Evaluation metrics for the SRM 2517a case study

| Metric | Estimate |
|--------|----------|
| Real IRR | 4,400% |
| Benefit-to-cost ratio | 267:1 |
| NPV using 1998 as base year in year 2000 dollars | $58.1 million |
| NPV using 2002 as base year in year 2000 dollars | $76.2 million |

The metrics in Table 6.4 reflect a portion of the social return on investments, and these are the returns that economists call producer surplus.
Producer surplus is the profit resulting because of the use of the infratech-
nology embodied in SRM 2517a. Although the estimate will be a rough
one, we are also able to provide a first-order approximation of the consumer
surplus gains as well. Figure 6.1 represents the situation for the typical
company selling a differentiated product that uses SRM 2517a in the production process.[10] The availability of the new standard reference material
lowers the unit costs as shown in the figure from "unit cost 2517" to "unit
cost 2517a." Consequently, the company chooses a lower price and sells
more of its product or service.[11] The company's profit maximizing price
falls from $P_1$ to $P_2$, and the optimal output increases from $Q_1$ to $Q_2$. The new
surplus – resulting because of the new lower unit costs of production
enabled by SRM 2517a – is the sum of the areas $A$, $B$, $C$, and $D$. Area $A$

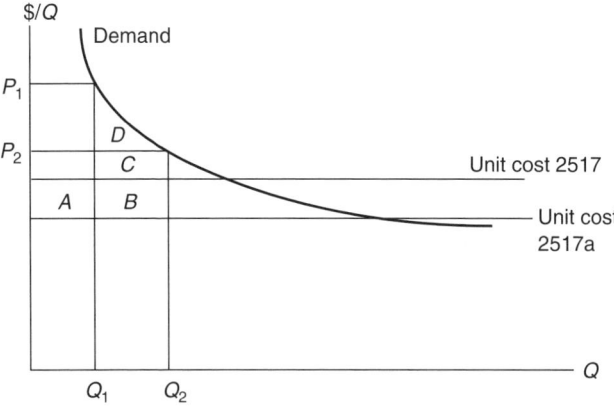

*Figure 6.1* Demand, unit cost, and net gain in producer and consumer surplus from the use of SRM 2517a.

*Table 6.5* Revised evaluation metrics for the SRM 2517a case study using total benefits (net gains in the total of producer surplus and consumer surplus) (year 2000 dollars)

| Metric | Estimate |
|---|---|
| Real IRR | 5,500% |
| Benefit-to-cost ratio | 331 : 1 |
| NPV using 1998 as the base year in year 2000 dollars | $72.0 million |
| NPV using 2002 as the base year in year 2000 dollars | $94.4 million |

represents the new producer surplus on sales of the original amount of output. Area B plus area C represents the new producer surplus from the sale of additional output. Finally, area D represents the net gain in consumer surplus (new consumer surplus that does not simply offset a loss in previously existing producer surplus).

Details about price, output and unit cost are considered highly confidential and the industry respondents were typically unwilling to provide such information. However, one of the respondents was willing to provide detailed information, for its own production, about $P_1$, $P_2$, $Q_1$, $Q_2$, and unit cost both before SRM 2517a was introduced and then after it replaced SRM 2517. For that company, the ratio of net new consumer surplus to new producer surplus, $D/(A + B + C)$, equals 0.238. That company conjectures that its experience with the cost lowering effect of replacing SRM 2517 with SRM 2517a would be similar to the experiences of others in the industry. Therefore, as a first-order approximation of consumer surplus gains because of the process innovations from applying SRM 2517a, we multiply the new producer profits – the industry benefits column of Table 6.3 – by 0.238. Table 6.5 recalculates the metrics for the SRM 2517a project by using the total of the net gains in producer and consumer surplus (the industrial benefits from Table 6.3 multiplied by 1.238) as the social return on the investment.

# 7 Case study of injectable composite bone grafts

The goal of this project was to develop a new bone graft material superior to any product currently available for dental or orthopedic surgeries.

## Background information and overview of the project[1]

The Polymers Division of the Materials Science and Engineering Laboratory has had a relationship with the American Dental Association (ADA) since 1928 through NIST's collaboration with the ADA's Health Foundation's (ADAHF) Paffenbarger Research Center (PRC).[2] Since early 1990, the Polymers Division has also enjoyed a research relationship with the National Institutes of Health (NIH), investigating the compatibility of new materials in the human body since the early 1990s.

In 1997, based on research in the Polymers Division sponsored by NIST, the National Institute of Dental and Craniofacial Research (NIDCR) of the NIH, and the ADAHF, a calcium phosphate cement was developed and introduced into the market by an ADAHF license under the name BoneSource®. According to the ADA:[3]

> This plaster-like material can be placed surgically, molded and sculpted to the correct anatomical shape, and will set to form a hard implant composed entirely of hydroxyapatite. The implant material is slowly dissolved and replaced entirely by new bone, thus repairing the original defect.

This material has successfully been used to repair cranial bone, but it has at least two problems that motivated Dr Wang's intramural project. One, the cement does not disappear quickly, meaning that the regeneration of new bone cells is slow. And two, the product could not be used in load-bearing areas in orthopedic surgeries.

In 1999, Dr Francis Wang in the Polymers Division began a 3-year ATP intramural project on the compatibility of new bone graft material in the human body. Dr Wang received $409,000 over 3 years allocated as FY 1999: $100,000, FY 2000: $150,000, FY 2001: $159,000.

A number of key issues were addressed in the intramural project. One issue was to develop an alternative bone graft material that was "resorbable" that is, the bone graft will dissolve away – referred to as "resorbing" the bone graft material. Another issue was to study additives that would rapidly regenerate new bone growth. Further, the material had to have enough mechanical integrity so that it would not migrate into the region outside of the area of the bone with a defect. And finally, the material needed to be biocompatible with the surrounding tissue.

Dr Wang found that tiny biodegradable polymer marbles that are 200–300 μm in diameter, called micro-spheres, could be mixed into calcium phosphate paste to occupy as much as 60 percent by volume to provide pores in which new bone cells can grow as the micro-spheres dissolve (over a 3-week period). The surgeon molds the paste into the defect, and the "marbles" disappear in about three weeks. While the micro-spheres are in the cement, they maintain the mechanical strength of the composite bone graft. Rather than encapsulate a growth factor protein in the micro-spheres, Dr Wang demonstrated that the protein can be dissolved in the liquid part of the cement paste (made from calcium phosphate powder and liquid). Also developed during this project was a process that speeds the release of the growth factor protein. This process is related to the amount and type of micro-sphere particles added to the cement mixture.

## Implications for industry and society

This ATP intramural project complemented the earlier research with NIDCR. Dr Wang's project, building on the extant knowledge in the field, developed a new bone graft material superior to any product currently available for dental or orthopedic surgeries. This product is compatible with the human body, maintains its integrity in that it does not migrate from the implanted area, and rapidly stimulates new bone growth. As a result, its use is expected to benefit patients by reducing the time, cost, and discomfort associated with dental implant surgery, certain periodontal surgeries, and certain orthopedic surgeries.

Based on Dr Wang's responses to the electronic survey, in the absence of the ATP intramural award, he would have undertaken a project with similar goals and milestones, as expected given that the project complemented on-going research in the Polymers Division. However, this project in comparison to the hypothetical project is broader in scope and thus took longer to complete, was more technically challenging, and is expected to lead to more technical papers, new measurement technologies, and new databases.

## Benefit and cost information[4]

From interviews it was learned that new enhanced calcium phosphate cements that use Dr Wang's research results are projected to be marketable by 2006 and anticipated to have long-term social benefits. Although research in the field is expected to continue between now and 2006, it is anticipated that additional research will not change the findings of Dr Wang's research and therefore will not diminish the social value of his findings or make them obsolete. According to Dr Eichmiller, Dr Wang's research could yield social benefits for as long as 30 years.

These new cement products are expected to yield the following benefits:

1 *Reduce the cost of dental implants by 30 percent*    The time between the implant and the mounting of a tooth crown is expected to be reduced from 6 to 2 months and hence the number of check-up visits with the oral surgeon will likewise be reduced; as a result, the respondents believe that costs will be reduced by 30 percent. Currently,[5] the average cost of a dental implant (not including the cost of the tooth crown) is between $1,500 and $1,800. In 2001, there were approximately 2.2 million implants in the United States.[6]

The value of the reduced cost of a dental implant beginning in 2006, as a result of Dr Wang's research, is an annual aggregate savings of $1.09 billion in year 2001 dollars. That is, because with implants currently costing on average $1,650 and a reduction in costs of 30 percent, the savings are $1.09 billion (0.30 × $1,650 × 2.2 million).

2 *Increase the success rate of periodontal surgeries*    There are currently two risks associated with periodontal surgeries (including osseous grafts and soft tissue grafts). The first risk, and this applies to orthopedic surgery, is associated with possible contamination from using freeze-dried cadaver bone from bone banks. The second risk is that the procedure will not be successful. At present, the success rate is between 60 percent and 70 percent, and the current average cost of a surgery is between $2,000 and $3,000. Whereas the enhanced calcium phosphate cement is not expected to reduce the cost of a procedure, it is expected to eliminate the risk of contamination and increase the success rate to between 80 and 90 percent. In 2001 there were an estimated 800,000 grafts for which the new cement could have been used and thus could have increased the success rate of the graft.[7]

No dollar value of the benefits from the increased success rate of periodontal surgeries is quantified. There is certainly a physical benefit to consumers from receiving medical benefits from a paid-for procedure; however, those we talked with in the field suggested that when a periodontal surgery fails the patient rarely has it redone. Thus, there is no explicit cost saving to consumers, and oral surgeons are not financially worse off absent any impact on reputation.

3 *Reduce recovery time from orthopedic surgeries*   Currently, ceramic phosphate cement is not used in load-bearing orthopedic surgeries because the recovery time is too long. At present, the turnover rate for bone regrowth is about 8 mm per year. The enhanced cement could be used in such surgeries and would decrease recovery time as well as post-recovery physical therapy time.

There is an explicit economic benefit to society from a recovering patient having less pain and suffering and being able to return sooner to productive work. However, absent information on the precise reduction in recovery time, the percentage of recovering patients who will return to work and the wage (marginal productivity) of those workers, this benefit is not quantified.

4 *Allow orthopedic procedures on joints to become closed procedures* On average, the fixture time to repair a joint fracture, a distal radius fracture (wrist) or a distal tibial pilon fracture (ankle), is between 6 and 8 weeks, and the average cost when surgery is needed for these fractures is between $6,000 and $10,000. This cost would fall by about 50 percent if a closed procedure were to be used, that is, if enhanced cement were to be injected into the fractured area as an alternative to surgery. In general, the cost of a closed orthopedic procedure is about one-half of one involving intervention. In 1999, there were 650,000 bone grafts, and a closed procedure would have been applicable on approximately 10–20 percent,[8] of the cases.

The cost to harvest a patient's own bone, typically about $1,000, could also be avoided with a closed procedure. To avoid possible contamination from freeze-dried bone from a bone bank, it is common during reconstructive orthopedic surgery for bone to be taken from the patient's iliac for use in the reconstruction.

The value of the reduced cost of an orthopedic procedure, using a closed procedure instead of invasive surgical intervention, can be estimated in year 2001 dollars in terms of 97,500 bone graft patients ($0.15 \times 650,000$) having saved, on average, $5,000 ($4,000 + $1,000). This translates to an annual aggregate savings of $487.5 million.

Based on the interview information, the following conservative assumptions underlie the timing of these economic benefits.

First, it is assumed that the enhanced bone cement will take one full year to penetrate the market. Those with whom we spoke who are currently involved in selling bone cement products (i.e. pharmaceutical representatives) and those who have knowledge of the various procedures in which the new product will be used, expected that the new product would penetrate the market in less than 6 months, based on their experience with the current bone cements that are available.

Second, the projected number of procedures referenced above for each category of consumer cost savings is not assumed to increase over time, although as noted the trend is certainly increasing.

Third, while there is the expectation that social benefits will extend well beyond 2016, future benefits for only 10 years are considered. Although at the time of this case study, Dr Wang's research results are authoritative and no new technological advances are forecast, forecasting future research results is not an exact science. Our discussions with Dr Wang and Dr Eichmiller led us to conclude that, absent ATP's support of this project, the private sector would not easily, if at all, have duplicated his results.[9] But since that assumption is conjecture, the inclusion of only 10 years of benefits removes any biases from our analysis that would be associated with that point given that if the private sector did eventually duplicate his results, it would have had to do so after the fact.

Costs potentially include ATP funding of Dr Wang's research project, plus expenses the industry will incur to develop and market the cement, plus medical practitioners' costs to use it. The three pharmaceutical representatives who offered insights about this cement – and all three were given all relevant publications – conveyed that their contacts in corporate R&D were of the opinion that once the product was on the market, companies would have to add little to it before marketing it.[10] When queried, the amount that each company reported expecting to add to market the product was "less than $250,000." Using $245,000 for total company marketing costs and assuming that each of the five pharmaceutical companies will allocate costs evenly over the years 2002–2006, the annual total costs by this industry segment to bring Dr Wang's research to market is $245,000.

The five surgeons with whom we spoke about this cement told us that it would be very easy to use and would likely be accompanied by a video training tape, thus making the learning time less than one hour. As this means that pull costs are relatively insignificant in this analysis, they are therefore ignored.

Table 7.1 compares the ATP allocations to fund Dr Wang's project in years 1999, 2000, and 2001 (converted from nominal values to year 2000 dollars) to the projected social benefits associated with savings from that project (in year 2000 dollars) with a one-year lag from 2006 to 2007 to account for the time needed for the new product to penetrate the market. These projected social benefits are, in our opinion, a combination of consumer and producer benefits.

*Table 7.1* Estimated total costs and estimated total social benefits associated with injectable composite bone grafts (year 2000 dollars)

| Year | ATP funds ($1,000s) | Private sector marketing costs ($1,000s) | Estimated social benefits ($billions) |
|------|------|------|------|
| 1999 | 102.3 | | |
| 2000 | 150.0 | | |
| 2001 | 155.8 | | |
| 2002 | | 245.0 | |
| 2003 | | 245.0 | |
| 2004 | | 245.0 | |
| 2005 | | 245.0 | |
| 2006 | | 245.0 | |
| 2007 | | | 1.55 |
| 2008 | | | 1.55 |
| 2009 | | | 1.55 |
| 2010 | | | 1.55 |
| 2011 | | | 1.55 |
| 2012 | | | 1.55 |
| 2013 | | | 1.55 |
| 2014 | | | 1.55 |
| 2015 | | | 1.55 |
| 2016 | | | 1.55 |

*Table 7.2* Evaluation metrics for the injectable composite bone graft case study

| Metric | Estimate |
|------|------|
| Real IRR | 230% |
| Benefit-to-cost ratio | 5,400 : 1 |
| NPV using 1999 as the base year in year 2000 dollars | $6.8 billion |
| NPV using 2002 as the base year in year 2000 dollars | $8.3 billion |

There are no a priori reasons to believe that the dental and surgical procedures described above occur in competitive markets, and no information was learned during our interviews to suggest that such was the case. Thus, some portion of the calculated benefits will be passed along to consumers and some portion will be retained as producer profits.

The impact of those benefits is expected to be extraordinarily large. Even if we knew the amounts of the investment costs for the follow-on research and included them in the metrics on the assumption that they were necessary for commercialization of Dr Wang's results, the social rate of return would be extraordinarily high.

## Results of the economic analysis

Table 7.2 summarizes the four evaluation metrics for this case study. Each was calculated using the data in Table 7.1.

Clearly, based on one or all of the metrics in the table above, the ATP intramural funded bone grafts project was successful from an economic perspective. The internal rate of return is 230 percent, the benefit-to-cost ratio is 5,400 : 1, and the NPV in 2002 in year 2000 dollars is over $8 billion.

# 8 Case study of Internet commerce for manufacturing

The goals of this project were to:

- assist industry in developing open standards to enable exchange of business and product data for all supply chain participants;
- provide a flexible testbed for industry and government to collaborate in testing and evaluating standards-based tools and integration technologies;
- demonstrate business-to-business (B2B) electronic commerce (e-commerce).

## Background information and overview of the project[1]

In 1998, Mr Thomas Rhodes in the Software Diagnostics and Conformance Testing Division of the ITL and Ms Barbara Goldstein in the Electricity Division of the EEEL began a 3-year cross-laboratory multi-researcher ATP intramural project to address problems facing companies that rely on the Internet for B2B e-commerce. More specifically, the Internet Commerce for Manufacturing (ICM) project focused on the printed circuit board fabrication and assembly manufacturing process and the industry and trading partners that are involved in the life cycle of the activities of manufacturing and assembling electronic boards. The other laboratories/groups with personnel involved in this project were the MEL and the Manufacturing Extension Partnership (MEP) Program. This group received $580,000 over three years allocated as FY 1998: $200,000, FY 1999: $230,000, FY 2000: $150,000.

At the time of the ATP intramural project proposal, original equipment manufacturers (OEMs) in the computer industry, such as Hewlett Packard, Intel, Lucent Technologies, and Motorola, were beginning to rely on contract manufacturers in the electronics manufacturing services (EMS) industry for the engineering and manufacturing of components to be used in printed circuit boards (PCBs).[2]

Because of this trend and its expected growth, and because of increased complexity and density of PCBs, industry was expressing great concern about the need for Web-based data sharing and for reliable mechanisms for the exchange of design and performance data. According to Mr Rhodes and Ms Goldstein, the IPC was aware of NIST's work on such standards as GenCAM (discussed below) through interaction with NIST scientists in RosettaNet,[3] a consortium of between 500 and 600 information technology companies worldwide.[4] Also, in 1998, the National Electronics Manufacturing Initiative (NEMI)[5] Technology Roadmap identified the lack of interoperability among applications in e-commerce as one of the greatest barriers for the industry of manufacturers of mechanical and electronic components, especially the small and medium-sized manufacturers.

The ATP intramural project was conceived by the two researchers as a response to OEM needs in particular. MEL's interest in the project stemmed from its interest in improving the manufacture of PCBs; ITL was interested in infrastructure and architecture issues to enable e-commerce; EEEL was interested in assisting industry to more efficiently form and maintain supply chain partnerships in order for the industry to best compete in the global marketplace; and, MEP was looking for solutions that could assist small and medium-sized companies become involved in e-commerce.

ICM had the same broad objectives as RosettaNet, but the objectives of the ICM project were focused farther downstream in the supply chain. The ICM project focused on the design and manufacturing of PCBs. RosettaNet's goal was to develop a set of Web-based standards for trading partners in the IT industry so that these companies could begin to engage in e-commerce.

ICM directly involves the PCBs assembly supply chain.[6] OEM companies at the bottom of the supply chain originate the product structure and feed it to the upstream partners. Once this process begins, various types of information – design for assembly, fabrication, test feedback and material status, work-in-progress, and quality information – flow back to the OEMs. Because OEMs will be feeding and receiving information from a number of external EMS companies, and perhaps some that are internal, OEMs need methods to interpret accurately the feedback information and to respond in a way that will be universally understood. This information exchange is complex, taking into account that EMS companies themselves have to interact with their suppliers, and often a given supplier services more than one EMS company. OEM and EMS companies are emphasized in this case study.

At the time that this project began, the initial version of GenCAM (IPC 2510) was about ready to be released. NIST played an important role in the promulgation of this standard, but that work was outside the ATP-funded

ICM project. The GenCAM standard described PCBs and their assembly in sufficient detail for designated boards to be manufactured and assembled by the EMS. GenCAM, however, did not facilitate high-level supply chain communication of business and product definition data.

The technical approach of the ICM project was to work closely with industry through standards development organizations and industry consortia to develop candidate standards, to test those standards in an open testbed, and to assess the feasibility of using such standards in conjunction with other standards (e.g. GenCAM).

All the objectives of the project were met and all the related activities have collectively benefited industry. The one activity that could clearly be isolated as a direct result of the ICM project, and thus became the evaluation focus of this study, is the formulation and adoption in November 2001 of the following Product Data eXchange (PDX) standards:

- IPC-2571, Generic Requirements for Electronics Manufacturing Supply Chain Communication.
- IPC-2576, Sectional Requirements for Electronics Manufacturing Supply Chain Communication of As-Build Product Data.
- IPC-2578, Sectional Requirements for Supply Chain Communication of Bill of Materials and Product Design Configuration Data.

The project also led to the IPC-2577 proposal for Sectional Requirements for the Supply Chain (B2B) Communication of Quantity Product Data, but our focus is exclusively on the PDX standards.[7]

Because the ICM project was initiated in part in response to the NEMI roadmap, and because NIST had previously helped to launch, manage, and contribute technically to the NEMI Virtual Factory Information Interchange Project (VFIIP), those involved in the ICM project were well positioned to design and complete the ICM project.

In addition, the project led to the adoption of a sectional GenCAM requirement, IPC-2511–19, and to a RosettaNet standard, PIPS 2C1–10. However, the remainder of this case study focuses only on the economic effects traceable to the PDX standards because that work is a stand-alone accomplishment that is directly traceable to the ICM project and can uniquely be identified by those in the industry.

## Implications for industry and society

Based on Mr Rhodes' and Ms Goldstein's responses to the electronic survey for the ICM team, this ATP-funded ICM project both complemented ongoing research activities at NIST – in the three separate laboratories represented in the project – and also fostered new initiatives in researching, developing, and testing new technology and specifications for e-commerce in manufacturing.

Ongoing NIST research traditionally involved development and testing of open standards and underlying technologies targeted toward improving software and systems integration and interoperability. The ICM project, however, focused on the emerging technologies and standards for e-commerce and their potential use toward improving supply-chain integration among companies engaged in the design and manufacture of electronic printed circuit boards and assemblies. Rather than simple catalog-based ordering over the Web (i.e. B2C), e-commerce for manufacturing involved more complex build-to-order processes, referred to as B2B e-commerce. The ICM project helped focus NIST efforts toward investigating technologies, such as XML, agent technology, ontologies, semantic resolution, distributed object models, etc., that could support the dynamic requirements of B2B e-commerce. Today, various projects within NIST laboratories (ITL, EEEL, MEL, BFRL, MEP) continue to pursue these research areas with an eye toward supporting e-commerce for manufacturing and assisting industry in developing specifications and tools based on suitable technologies.

Without ATP funding, it is highly unlikely that the goals and milestones of the ICM project ever would have been funded. Efforts were made to secure funding from the NIST National Advanced Manufacturing Testbed (NAMT) project, which endorsed the ICM project, but which did not have available funds to support ICM. Further, until ATP funding was obtained, internal laboratory funding was also unavailable. Hence, ATP funding made the ICM project feasible.

PDX standards have the potential to affect three levels of the supply chain: OEMs, EMS companies, and the EMS suppliers. Only the first two levels of the supply chain are considered in the analysis that follows. There is a pragmatic reason for delimiting the levels of analysis. Based on telephone interviews with industry experts,[8] at most 2–3 percent of the component suppliers' industries are just beginning to use aspects of the PDX standards that were approved in November 2001. Component suppliers are at the level in the supply chain expected by EMS companies to increase conformance over time. These EMS suppliers could not approximate the benefits from PDX standards since the EMS-to-supplier interface for the most part has not yet begun to embrace the use of all of the PDX standards.

The consensus expressed in telephone interviews with industry experts is that OEMs and EMS companies not only were the first in the supply chain to use the standards, but also began to realize cost-saving benefits from the PDX standards even before they were finalized by the IPC.

**Benefit and cost information**

The benefits quantified in this case study reflect cost savings because the companies received the benefits of the PDX standards developed in the ATP project sooner than if they had evolved from industry's initiatives. The consensus opinion expressed by individuals interviewed at OEM companies was that cost-savings were realized by both OEM and EMS companies beginning in 2001.

For OEMs:

- The average cost savings per interviewed OEM, in terms of man-years saved because of improved communication with contractors in 2001, was 2–3 man-years of savings, where a fully burdened man-year is valued at $225,000, for an average major OEM savings of $562,500 ($225,000 $\times$ 2.5 man-years) (in year 2001 dollars).

- At the time of the interviews, only the major OEMs were using the PDX standards for communication with the EMS industry, so a conservative estimate of cost-savings for the $500 billion (in year 2001 dollars) OEM industry could be derived by using a multiple of 10 (i.e. 10 major OEMs). Over time, other OEMs would certainly adopt the PDX standards, but no estimates were given for the rate of diffusion of the standard. Therefore, benefits are conservatively estimated under the assumption that the adopting population equals the 10 major OEMs.

- NIST's role through the activities of the ICM project hastened the promulgation and adoption of the PDX standards by the OEMs by at least 2 years. The OEMs are of the opinion that absent NIST's role, the adoption of the PDX standards would have been delayed by at least 2 years from the date of the interviews, meaning that benefits could have been realized in 2004.[9] Thus, benefits from the ICM project to OEMs were and are expected to be realized in years 2001, 2002, and 2003. These benefits (in year 2001 dollars) per year are $5.625 million ($562,500 $\times$ 10 OEMs).

- OEMs did not have an opinion as to how long the PDX standard will last. To be conservative, we truncate benefits to OEMs at year 2004 and measure only the benefits resulting from the acceleration of the PDX standards caused by NIST's funding.

For EMS companies:

- The average interviewed EMS cost savings was 1–1.5 man-years per year. This estimate was derived on the basis of 200–300 man-hours saved on data translations per customer for each of, on average,

10 major customers. Thus, each EMS using the PDX standards saved 2,000–3,000 man-hours in 2001. Using the suggested fully-burdened rate of $175,000 for a fully-burdened man-year in the EMS industry, the average savings was $218,750 ($175,000 × 1.25 man-years) (in year 2001 dollars).

• At the time of the interview, only about 10 percent of the $180 billion domestic EMS industry was using the PDX standards, but this percentage is expected to increase over time as the EMS industry is forecast to grow at 25 percent per year.[10]

• A conservative estimate for cost-savings to the EMS industry can be derived by using a multiple of 5, for the five major contractors. While smaller EMS companies are adopting the PDX standards, these five are ahead of the curve. These benefits (in year 2001 dollars) per year were $1.094 million ($218,750×5 EMS companies).

• NIST's role through the activities of the ICM project hastened the promulgation and adoption of the PDX standards by the EMS industry. Absent NIST, such standards would eventually have been promulgated from the EMS side, but not until at least 5 years from the date of the interviews.[11]

• Those interviewed in the EMS industry are of the opinion, averaged from all responses, that benefits from the adoption of the PDX standards will last at least 8–10 years. Thus, benefits from the ICM project to the EMS industry were and are conservatively expected to be realized for only 8 years – 2001 through 2008 – and are reasonably projected farther out than benefits to the OEM industry.[12]

*Table 8.1* Estimated total costs and estimated total social benefits associated with ICM (year 2000 dollars)

| Year | ATP funds ($1,000s) | Estimated social benefits ($1,000s) |
|------|---------------------|-------------------------------------|
| 1998 | 207.4 | — |
| 1999 | 235.2 | — |
| 2000 | 150.0 | — |
| 2001 | — | 6,580 |
| 2002 | — | 6,580 |
| 2003 | — | 6,580 |
| 2004 | — | 1,080 |
| 2005 | — | 1,080 |
| 2006 | — | 1,080 |
| 2007 | — | 1,080 |
| 2008 | — | 1,080 |

*Table 8.2* Evaluation metrics for the Internet commerce for
manufacturing case study

| Metric | Estimate |
|---|---|
| Real IRR | 220% |
| Benefit-to-cost ratio | 33:1 |
| NPV using 1998 as the base year in year 2000 dollars | $17.7 million |
| NPV using 2002 as the base year in year 2000 dollars | $23.2 million |

Costs included in the analysis were limited to ATP funds. None of those
interviewed experienced significant pull costs associated with adopting the
PDX standards.

Table 8.1 compares the ATP allocations to the ICM project in years 1998,
1999, and 2000 to the projected social benefits associated with savings from
that project. All estimates are in year 2000 dollars.

## Results of the economic analysis

Table 8.2 summarizes the four evaluation metrics for this case study. Each
was calculated using the data in Table 8.1.

Clearly, based on one or all of the metrics in the table above, the ATP
intramural-funded ICM project was successful from an economic perspective.
The internal rate of return is 220 percent, the benefit-to-cost ratio is 33:1,
and the NPV in 2002 (in year 2000 dollars) is $23 million.

# 9 Case study of polymer composite dielectrics for integrated thin-film capacitors

The goals of this project were to establish new metrology to characterize electrical properties of embedded capacitance in printed wiring boards and advance knowledge about the limits of this new system.

## Background information and overview of the project[1]

In 1999, Dr Jan Obrzut in the Polymers Division of the Materials Science and Engineering Laboratory began a 3-year ATP intramural research project to develop knowledge about the electrical properties of thin-film polymer composite dielectric materials[2] used as embedded capacitance[3] for printed wiring boards. Dr Obrzut received $260,000 over three years allocated as FY 1999: $70,000, FY 2000: $70,000, and FY 2001: $120,000.

This research project grew from the needs of industry for new thin-film embedded passive materials, fabrication processes that are compatible with the new printed circuit boards with embedded capacitance, and broadband testing of the materials at frequencies of 500 MHz to 10 GHz.

The project successfully met its three objectives:

1 to advance measurement science by developing a technique for testing the microwave broadband permittivity of dielectric films with a high dielectric constant;[4]
2 to develop the practical application important for industry of broadband impedance[5] characterization of dielectric films for embedded capacitance;
3 to contribute to materials science by developing fundamental understanding of high frequency dielectric properties in polymer-ferroelectric ceramic composites.[6]

Dielectric films can be used in the new packaging solutions for the high-performance chips combining resistors, capacitors, and microstrips with integrated circuits in printed circuit boards. The new solutions provide the necessary terminations, decoupling, and interconnects for the operation of broadband high-frequency communications systems. The embedded capacitance, using dielectric films with high dielectric constants and low dielectric loss, allows the systems to operate at high frequencies by providing a low impedance power plane.[7] The embedded capacitance also reduces the space taken by capacitors, allowing miniaturization or additional features and hence more functionality from the board.

The low impedance of the power plane is the essential requirement for microwave packaging. A key problem in microwave processing currently is that every interconnection creates more impedance. To address the need for low impedance of the power plane with embedded capacitance, industry is looking for new dielectric composite materials.

## Implications for industry and society

The new technology developed in the intramural project allows characterization of the embedded capacitance used for decoupling (i.e. decreasing power plane impedance) and that capacitance is needed in the high-speed electronics used in the transmission of information in communications systems. At the time that the ATP-funded project was concluding in 2001, the customers for the resistors, capacitors, and dielectrics used for interconnects included GSM Global System for Mobile Communications (the European standard) then operating at 900 MHz (and migrating to 1.8 GHz), Digital Cordless Standard (also European) GSM 1800 operating in the 1.8 GHz range (and migrating to 3.6 GHz), and iDEN Integrated Digital Enh. Network (a Motorola standard, US) operating at 800 MHz, 900 MHz, and 1.5 GHz (and migrating to 3.0 GHz) bands.

All of those applications were developed based on functional testing – there was an iterative process, then the dielectrics were tuned, and finally the functional performance was developed. In the iterative process of functional testing, the communications between materials suppliers and users were not well informed. They did not talk the same language, because the consumers, the device producers, did not know what to say about the dielectric constant they required, and the materials providers did not know what to provide. There was no testing procedure to bridge the different languages used by the materials suppliers and the materials users.

Dr Obrzut's research has provided the needed procedure and a base of knowledge about the properties of the materials. For these reasons, the ATP intramural project has had important impacts on industry.

NIST has been a member of the Embedded Decoupling Capacitance (EDC) Industrial Consortium that framed the theory and the applications and the measurement science for integrated passive devices embodying embedded capacitance. The consortium has met frequently and regularly beginning in 1997, and the outputs of the ATP intramural research project informed the work of the consortium. Industry formulated what was needed – passive devices providing low-impedance power planes. NIST showed that polymer composites have the properties industry needs. NIST provided accurate high frequency permittivity and impedance characteristics data for several dielectric films with high dielectric constants that were developed by industry for the embedded decoupling capacitance applications in high-speed electronics. The dielectric films for which NIST provided characteristics data include 3M's C-Ply, HADCO's EmCap, and DuPont's HiK.

NIST's research also led to the discovery that an embedded capacitance layer made of polymer composites with high dielectric constants can provide the desired low impedance characteristic better than any other known packaging solution for the high performance chips combining resistors, capacitors, and microstrips with integrated circuits in printed circuit boards to provide the necessary terminations, decoupling, and interconnects for the operation of broadband high-frequency communications systems. Also, in the ATP intramural project, NIST initiated work on a new IPC standard dielectric test method in the range of 100 MHz to 10 GHz. The NIST work is in the public domain; everyone can look at the work and benefit from it.

The ATP-funded project for NIST complemented and accelerated the research agenda of the Polymers Division. Dr Obrzut described its impact[8] on industry as follows:

This program was within the laboratory mission to initiate and expand its research capabilities on dielectric properties of organic polymers and composites at microwave frequencies.[9] The program started in 1999 and concluded in 2001. As a result, we developed a new broadband testing methodology for dielectric films. Subsequently, we discovered and then characterized a high frequency relaxation process in polymer composites, which is important for practical applications. Since the method enables measurements at microwave frequencies, it is attractive for both the industry and academic research.

## Benefit and cost information[10]

Discussions with industry reveal several categories of benefits, most of which are potential benefits because the embedded capacitance technology is still being developed. The categories for industrial benefits from the ATP-funded dielectrics project are materials characterization savings, improved production yields and negotiation cost savings, and the enabling of new products.

Once the new IPC dielectric test standard is ready and the embedded capacitance technology fully developed, industry expects benefits to result from being able to characterize the materials and better understand their performance at high frequencies in developing materials for OEMs. At that time, the benefits would be quantified as lower costs for materials suppliers characterizing dielectric materials and for board fabricators verifying the performance of materials. Further, the test method is expected to result in accurate characterization of materials allowing higher production yields for both materials suppliers and the board fabricators. Finally, the test method will enable new products for the materials suppliers, the board manufacturers, and the OEMs as the embedded capacitance technology becomes a commercial reality.

Industry respondents reported that the impact of Dr Obrzut's research to date has been on materials suppliers. The materials suppliers have benefited in that they can now effectively communicate about the performance characteristics of the materials in high frequency applications. Industry experts expect the commercial lifetime of the thin-film dielectric materials and the testing methodology to characterize them to be at least 20–25 years.

1  *Materials characterization savings*   Dr Obrzut's test method will reduce the costs of characterizing materials. Instead of relying on trial and error, the test will give accurate information about the properties of dielectric materials being used.[11] There are two important aspects. First, the new metrology allows industry to understand clearly the performance of the materials themselves. With the other existing methods, the characterization of the performance of the thin film dielectric materials is not adequate in certain frequency ranges of interest. Second, when a printed circuit board is designed, designers will have more information about what performance to expect once the material is in a board. In the past, designers have relied on the materials' performance characteristics when tested at low frequencies. The actual performance of the materials once in the board and operating at high frequencies was unknown.[12]

The supply chain of interest here is: materials suppliers, board fabricators, and then OEMs. Only those in the first two stages of the supply chain will realize materials characterization savings from the test method. OEMs will be measuring board characteristics from the surface of the board, so a different test will be used.[13]

2 *Production yield increases and negotiation cost savings*  The production yield of board fabricators and OEMs will increase with Dr Obrzut's test method in place and thus their production costs will decrease. Similarly, performance disputes among materials suppliers, board fabricators, and OEMs will decrease again decreasing production costs.[14]

3 *Enabling new products*  Dr Obrzut's test method will enable industry to move forward into new products with higher frequencies, enabling broader bandwidth communications technology with greater output flow. As a result, future sales will increase.[15]

Technology to use embedded capacitance is still being developed; therefore, it was not possible to obtain *separate* quantitative estimates of each of the categories of benefits from our respondents in industry. Instead, we are able to make a conservative estimate of the aggregate of the average annual benefits using a different approach. We asked the respondents how much they would have invested in the project if NIST had not been involved; their response became the basis for estimating a lower bound for what industry expected the benefits of the project to be.

Table 9.1 provides the time series for the costs of the ATP intramural dielectrics project (in year 2000 dollars). Respondents were asked to estimate any "pull costs." Such costs are initial costs, over and above any fees paid to NIST for the outputs of the NIST research, required to make use of the new test method in a company. The pull costs are one-time costs incurred prior to the in-house use of the test method. Discussions with industry show that there were essentially no discernable pull costs for industry because the new knowledge was assimilated in the course of the ongoing work of the EDC consortium members. However, industry did make in-kind contributions to Dr Obrzut's research project, contributing equipment, materials, and expertise of industry experts. Industry respondents estimated that those in-kind contributions through the EDC consortium were worth $1,345,000.[16] The costs for those in-kind contributions have been spread throughout the three years of the NIST project in the proportion of the annual NIST costs for the project. Thus, for 1999, 2000, and 2001, NIST's costs (in year 2000 dollars) were $71,600, $70,000,

*Table 9.1* Estimated total costs and social benefits associated with the developed
          test method (year 2000 dollars)

| Year | Costs ($1,000s) | Lower-bound expected benefits ($1,000s) |
|------|------|------|
| 1999 | 71,600 + 371,535 = 443.135 | |
| 2000 | 70,000 + 363,233 = 433.233 | |
| 2001 | 117,600 + 610,231 = 727.831 | |
| 2002 | — | |
| 2003 | — | |
| 2004 | — | 1,380 |
| . | — | . |
| . | | . |
| . | | . |
| 2020 | — | 1,380 |

and $117,600, respectively. The costs for the in-kind contributions from
industry are then $371,535, $363,233, and $610,231 for 1999, 2000, and
2001, respectively.

Also shown in Table 9.1 are lower bounds for the aggregated estimates
for the expected benefits to industry at the time that the investments in
the project were made. The benefits from being able to accurately characterize the dielectric materials, higher production yields, reduced negotiation costs, and enabling new products are potentially large but as yet,
are unrealized. However, we are able to make a conservative estimate of
the average annual benefits. In Table 9.1, our estimate for those potential unrealized benefits is indicated as $1,380,000 for the expected average
annual profits beginning in 2004 and lasting conservatively until
2020 (respondents indicated an expected commercial lifetime for the
embedded passive devices technology of at least 20–25 years). These
expected benefits begin in 2004 based on the report of well-informed
respondents.[17]

The expected average annual profits reported in the table were derived
based on industry responses to a hypothetical investment decision.
Discussions were conducted with knowledgeable respondents about what
would have happened if NIST had not funded Dr Obrzut's project. Under
that scenario, it is reasonable to assume that – given the market conditions
and expectations at the time when the NIST project began – beginning in
2000, each of the four prominent materials suppliers that participated in the
EDC consortium individually would have invested the amounts that were
invested in the NIST project. Thus, for the four suppliers together there

would have been $1,772,540, $1,732,932, and $2,911,324 invested in 2000, 2001, and 2002, respectively. In return, future profits would be expected to flow from 2004 through 2020.

To make the investment, industry would have required that the future profits be sufficient for the investment to return a yield exceeding a hurdle rate. The lower that hurdle rate, the lower the expected future profits would need to be for the investment to be worthwhile for industry. From work with industry, it is known (Link and Scott, 2001a) that for risky R&D investments, industry typically would require a much higher hurdle rate than the 7 percent real rate recommended by OMB as the opportunity cost of public funds. We conservatively apply a hurdle rate of 15 percent, and ask what average annual expected profits would have had to be over the years 2004 through 2020 to yield a 15 percent rate of return on the investments that industry would have made absent the NIST dielectrics project.

That average annual expected profit for the industry is $1,380,000 (in year 2000 dollars), and it is shown in Table 9.1 as annual benefits. Note that those average annual expected profits are just a bare minimum, lower bound on what expected profits would have been, since the estimated amount is just barely enough for the hurdle rate to be reached, and further the hurdle rate is a very conservative one that surely underestimates the one that industry would have used. Actual expected annual profits would surely have been much greater. They have not been realized to date, however, so the conservative, lower-bound estimate of $1,380,000 for the average annual profits is used.

## Results of the economic analysis

Table 9.2 summarizes the four evaluation metrics for this case study. Each was calculated using the aggregate data in Table 9.1.

*Table 9.2* Evaluation metrics for the dielectrics case study

| Metric | Estimate |
| --- | --- |
| Real IRR | 35% |
| Benefit-to-cost ratio | 7 : 1 |
| NPV using 1999 as the base year in year 2000 dollars | $8.8 million |
| NPV using 2002 as the base year in year 2000 dollars | $10.8 million |

The metrics for this particular case are necessarily – because of the special procedure used to estimate benefits – based on an educated guess about the lower bound for expected benefits.[18] Even using that lower bound, the project appears successful from an economic perspective. The internal rate of return is 35 percent, the benefit-to-cost ratio is 7:1, and the NPV in 2002 using in year 2000 dollars is $10.8 million.

# 10 Alternative evaluation templates

As we stated in Chapter 1, our purpose in writing this book was to present what is, to our knowledge, the first systematic study of a public agency's intramural research program. As such, we believe that our efforts as described herein, may be a template for others to follow.

The quantitative analysis based on our survey of NIST PIs is straightforward from an econometric point of view, and the findings do not need to be summarized in this final chapter.

The case studies, however, warrant further comment. The case studies were evaluated herein using what we have called the traditional evaluation method pioneered by Griliches and Mansfield. Using their methodology, we asked and answered the following relevant evaluation question: Given investment costs and the social benefits, what is the social rate of return to the innovation described in each case study?

There are two other evaluation methods, which from our experience may be more appropriate when evaluating the public sector's role in supporting the creation and distribution of new knowledge. We describe these evaluation methods in the following section, not to dismiss the relevance of the Griliches–Mansfield approach selected for the case studies herein, but rather for completeness should others use this book as a guide and template.

## The counterfactual evaluation method

When publicly funded publicly performed investments are being evaluated, holding constant the economic benefits that the Griliches–Mansfield model measures, and making no attempt to measure that stream, the relevant counterfactual question to ask is: What would the private sector have had to invest to achieve those same benefits in the absence of the public sector's investments?

The answer to this question reveals the benefits from the public sector, rather than the private sector, performing the investments. The counterfactual method measures as benefits the private sector's costs avoided through the public's investments plus the benefits from the public sector's investments that industry would be unable or unwilling to duplicate.[1] With those benefits – obtained in practice through extensive interviews with administrators, federal research scientists, and those in the private sector that would have to duplicate the investments (i.e. research) in the absence of public performance – counterfactual rates of return and benefit-to-cost ratios can be calculated. Those metrics answer the fundamental evaluation question: Are the public investments a more efficient way of generating the technology than private sector investments would have been?

The answer to this question aligns with the public accountability issues implicit in government mandates for accountability such as the US Government Performance and Results Act (GPRA) of 1993, and certainly addresses a key question of public sector stakeholders, who may doubt the appropriateness of government having a role in the innovation process in the first place.

## The spillover evaluation method

There are important projects where economic performance can be improved with public funding of privately performed research. Public funding is needed when socially valuable projects would not be undertaken without it. If the expected private rate of return from a research project falls short of the required rate called the hurdle rate, then the private sector firm will not invest in the project. Nonetheless, if the benefits of the research spill over to consumers and to firms other than the ones investing in the research, the social rate of return may exceed the appropriate hurdle rate. It would then be socially valuable to have the investments made, but since the private investors will not make them, the public sector should. By providing some public funding, thereby reducing the investment amount needed from the private firm or firms doing the research, the expected private rate of return can be increased above the hurdle rate. Thus, because of this subsidy, the private firm is willing to perform the research, which is socially desirable because much of its output spills over to other firms and sectors in the economy.

The question asked in the spillover method is one that facilitates an economic understanding of whether the public sector should be underwriting a portion of private-sector firms' research, namely: What proportion of the total profit stream *generated by the private firm's R&D and innovation* does the private firm expect to capture; and hence, what proportion is not appropriated but is instead captured by other firms that imitate the innovation or use knowledge generated by the R&D to produce competing products for the social good? The part of the stream of expected profits captured by the innovator is its private return, while the entire stream is the lower bound on the social rate of return. In essence, this method weighs the private return, estimated through extensive interviews with firms receiving public support about their expectations of future patterns of events and future abilities to appropriate R&D-based knowledge, against private investments. Then, the social rate of return weighs the social returns against the social investments.[2]

The application of the spillovers model to the evaluation of public funding/ private performance of research is appropriate since the output of the research is only partially appropriable by the private firm with the rest spilling over to society. The extent of the spillover of such knowledge with public good characteristics determines whether or not the public sector should fund or partially fund the research.

# Notes

## 1 Introduction

1 The term "generic technology" does not have a generally accepted definition. It is not a National Science Foundation reporting category of R&D spending (Link, 1996c). Tassey (1992, pp. 98–99) offers the following definition: "generic technology research is a major step in the sequential evolution of a typical industrial technology. It is the organization of scientific principles into a *functional technical concept*."

2 http://www.atp.nist.gov/atp/imp_fact.htm

3 The reader will note in Chapter 4 that we have presented detailed statistical results along with complete interpretations for those results. Our experience in conducting program evaluations, preparing reports, and later interpreting our findings to others, has been that the level of interest in statistical methodology and the idiosyncrasies of statistical results – especially those results that play only a supporting role – is sometimes wanting. All results are reported in Chapter 4 for completeness and, we hope, as a template for others to follow.

4 In addition to these research laboratories, *Technology Services* provides a variety of products and services to US industry such as Standard Reference Materials, Standard Reference Data, and Weights and Measures.

5 The Computer Systems Laboratory (CSL) and the Computing and Applied Mathematics Laboratory (CAML) were combined on February 16, 1997 to form the ITL. For purposes of inter-laboratory comparisons, pre-1997 information on these two MSLs is reported under the ITL.

6 In their explanation of the evaluations of public R&D investments from ATP's perspective and experience, Ruegg and Feller (2003) discuss outputs and outcomes from a broad assessment perspective. Tassey (2003) also provides such perspective. These sources give examples of outputs: contributions to underlying science, developed generic technology or infrastructure technology, documented use in industry of generic technology or infrastructure technology, intellectual property, and the promulgation of industry standards. They also provide examples of outcomes: industry R&D investment decisions, market access and entry decisions, industry cycle time, productivity, market penetration of new technology, product quality, product and systems reliability, reduced transaction costs. Further, they discuss and provide examples of the measurement of the social benefits – the impacts.

## 2 The role of public research institutions

1 Much of the material in this chapter draws from our previous writings, as noted explicitly throughout this chapter. Those writings were recently summarized, although within a different context, in Link and Scott (2004b).

2 The conceptual importance of identifying market failure for policy is also emphasized, although without any operational guidance, in Office of Management and Budget (1996).

3 Although Arrow does not elaborate on indivisibilities and inappropriability in his paper, the concepts are well understood in the innovation literature. Recalling that Arrow defines innovation "as the production of knowledge" (1962, p. 609), the market does not price knowledge in discrete bundles and thus because of such indivisibilities market prices may not send appropriate signals for economic units to make marginal decisions correctly. In the following sections, we discuss inappropriability and uncertainty.

4 There are two parts to the answer to the twin questions of how the social hurdle rate is determined and why it is represented as being less than the private hurdle rate. The first is grounded in the practice of evaluations, and the second is grounded in the theory of public policies to address market failure.

1 Regarding practice, for the case studies described in later chapters, the U.S. Office of Management and Budget has mandated that we use a specified real rate of return as the rate for evaluation studies, that is, the rate to be considered the opportunity cost for the use of the public funds in the investment projects we evaluate. The Office of Management and Budget (1992, p. 9) has said that: "Constant-dollar benefit–cost analyses of proposed investments and regulations should report net present value and other outcomes determined using a real discount rate of 7 percent." That real rate of return (and the related nominal rates derived by accounting for expected inflation rates in various periods of analysis) has been far less than what the respondents in the case studies told us is the private hurdle rate for comparable investment projects in industry during comparable time periods for the public investments we have studied.

2 Regarding theory, when we evaluate public investment projects, we are invariably looking at cases where there has been some sort of market failure. To improve upon the market solution, the government has become involved (in a variety of ways, in practice) with an investment project. Just as market solutions for the prices of goods may not reflect the social costs for the goods (because of market failure stemming from market power, imperfect information, externalities, or public goods), the private hurdle rates that reflect market solutions for the price of funds – the opportunity cost of funds to the private firms – may not reflect the social cost of the funds. The government may decide that the appropriate social cost – the opportunity cost for the public funds to be invested – differs from the market solution. Typically, in practice, the government believes that it faces less risk than the private sector firms doing similar investments; hence it will believe a lower yield is satisfactory since the public is bearing less risk than the private sector firm going it alone with a similar investment. More generally, government must decide what the opportunity costs of its public funds will be in various uses, and in general that will not be the same as the market

rate. However, all that said, clearly we know from Arrow's thinking about social choice that the government's decision about what the rate should be cannot possibly reflect the diversity of opinion in the private sector regarding the decision (Arrow, 1963). Consequently, as a logical matter, one could not prove that the government's choice of the right hurdle rate is obviously correct because diversity of opinion about the correct rate will not be reflected in the government's choice.

5  As Arrow (1962) explained, investments in knowledge entail uncertainty of two types – technical and market. The technical and market results from technology may be very poor, or perhaps considerably better than the expected outcome. Thus, a firm is justifiably concerned about the risk that its R&D investment will fail, technically or for any other reason. Or, if technically successful, the R&D investment output may not pass the market test for profitability. Further, the firm's private expected return typically falls short of the expected social return as previously discussed. This concept of downside risk is elaborated upon in Link and Scott (2001a).

6  See Leyden and Link (1999) on the role of a federal laboratory as an honest broker.

7  See David (1987) for detailed development of the ideas of path dependency in the context of business strategies and public policy toward innovation and diffusion of new technologies.

8  Tassey (1992, 1997, 2005) has developed and applied the idea of barriers to innovation and technology, using the idea to advance knowledge about appropriate technology policy for the US NIST.

9  Industry's scientists and engineers frequently interact with scientists in the public research institution in conferences and workshops and together they enable the public research laboratories to develop the standards needed as the technological requirements for industry to remain competitive evolve. See the several examples described in Link and Scott (2004b).

10  Private organizations with some public funding have evidently been successful in transferring technology to smaller businesses. Although coordinated by a public research institution, there is substantial private funding for the Malcolm Baldrige National Quality Award Program through NIST. The Program is focused on improving management and competitiveness. The pattern of shared funding among government and private organizations is common to many of the activities of public research institutions – most prominently activities largely performed by the private sector with oversight from the public institution and with some partial public funding of the projects (see Link and Scott, 2001b, forthcoming).

11  See Link and Scott (2001a).

## 4  Quantitative analysis of the effects of ATP intramural funding

1  A priori, pre-1997 projects might have different publication rates, other things being the same, because in 1997 the focus of the intramural awards program changed from supporting specific external projects to supporting more broad based projects. The pre-1997 respondents reported somewhat more publications per project than the respondents for later years. However, once the complete model with response effects is estimated, the publication

rates for the pre-1997 period and the subsequent years are, *ceteris paribus*, essentially the same.

2  The number of awards is also the number of survey instruments that the PI was asked to complete, and that number is expected to measure the difficulty that the PI faced in responding to the survey.

3  The budget figures were converted to constant 1996 dollars using CEA (2002), Table B7, "Chain-type price indexes for gross domestic product, 1959–2001." The index numbers, 1996 = 100, for gross domestic product were used.

4  Not all questions were answered on all returned surveys. This applies in particular to Q5. Information collected in Q7 and Q8 is not analyzed quantitatively.

5  The probabilities are predicted from the maximum likelihood probit model with selection – "heckprob" as described in StataCorp (2001, Vol. 2, pp. 31–39).

6  The predictions are made using the "pmargin" option for predictions (StataCorp, 2001, Vol. 2, p. 31).

7  A priori, one might expect that pre-1997 projects' publication rates would differ from the publication rates for projects in subsequent years. The focus of the intramural awards program changed in 1997 from supporting specific external projects to supporting more broad based projects. While the 179 reporting projects averaged 5.01 publications each with standard deviation 9.2 and range from 0 to 62, the 82 pre-1997 projects averaged 6.1 publications each with standard deviation 11.6 and a range from 0 to 62, and the 97 reporting projects from 1997 onward averaged 4.1 publications each with standard deviation 6.4 and a range from 0 to 46. However, in the model of publications with control for other variables and for sample selection, the publication rates for the older projects and the more recent ones are, *ceteris paribus*, essentially the same.

8  The latest version of LIMDEP has included the program to estimate models for count data with a correction for sample selection. See Greene (2002, p. WN-9): "The Poisson and negative binomial models can be fit with a correction for sample selection.... Estimation of the selection model is done by full information maximum likelihood...." We use the full information maximum likelihood model for the negative binomial models with selection estimated in this chapter.

9  An explanation of the model and the results are available from the authors.

10  See StataCorp (2001, Vol. 2, pp. 31–39).

11  See StataCorp (2001, Vol. 2, pp. 15–30).

## 5  Case study selection and methodology

1  Since these case studies were completed, ATP has combined these three technical offices into two.

2  While documentable technical outputs with socially valuable industrial applications were the criteria upon which the PMs were to recommend projects, in some instances the PM was not sufficiently familiar with the outcomes and impacts of the project after ATP funding ended to make a judgment as informed as we could make after our detailed interviews.

3  The GPRA of 1993 required that public institutions' research programs identify outputs and quantify the economic benefits of the outcomes associated with such outputs. Some public agencies have skirted the issue by arguing that the research they do or that they fund is peer reviewed, and thus it is sound; and if the research is sound, it must be socially valuable. Many embrace the

importance of having research peer reviewed both at the pre-funding stage as well as upon completion. However, the peer review process certainly does not address in any precise or reliable way whether or not the research is socially valuable from an economic standpoint. It is not so much that a formal analysis of social economic rates of return is officially out of bounds for the peer review process; rather, such an analysis is simply not a part of the peer review process as it currently exists. Other public agencies are attempting to be more exact in their approach to meeting the GPRA requirement to quantify outcomes' benefits. However, the hurdle that is difficult for most public agencies to clear is how to quantify benefits in a methodologically sound and defensible way.

4 The origin of this assumption can be traced at least to Bush (1945), although Link and Scott (1998, 2001a) have placed this assumption in a specific policy context.

5 Link and Scott have developed, through ongoing evaluations of federal research programs, an alternative approach to the *economic* evaluation of publicly funded research. This approach differs from traditional evaluation methods that have been used. The alternative approach is needed to provide additional insights because the traditional evaluation methods are limited in a GPRA world that is performance accountable. The genesis of this approach is in Link (1996a), and recent applications are in Link (1996b) and Link and Scott (1998) where a methodological chapter compares the alternative to the traditional evaluation methods. Link and Scott, and others, have used this approach in a number of the evaluation studies sponsored by the Program Office at NIST, as well as in several ATP-sponsored projects. The alternative approach and another alternative, originally developed in Link and Scott (2001a), are discussed in Chapter 10.

6 As relevant, other investment costs will be discussed in the case studies. Such investment costs are costs that the private sector will incur to utilize the ATP project's output. These are, stated differently, the costs incurred by the private sector to pull in ATP's output and utilize it efficiently. Hence, these costs are referred to as pull costs.

7 Of course, it is assumed that the benefit information provided by interviewed individuals is accurate and reproducible should subsequent interviews by others take place.

8 See CEA (2002), Table B7. The index number for 2001 was estimated as the average of the three quarterly observations available.

9 The characterization of the three metrics follows Link and Scott (1998).

10 Using the constant dollar figures for costs and benefits, the internal rate of return is a "real" rate of return. In contrast, some economic impact assessments (including many conducted for NIST's Program Office) have presented "nominal" rates of return that were based on time series of current dollars (the dollars of the year in which the benefits were realized or the costs were incurred).

11 With multiple reversals in the signs for the periodic net benefits, there can be multiple, real, positive solutions for $i$. However, in those cases, appropriate procedures are available to determine an appropriate, unique solution (see, e.g. Link and Scott, 1998, p. 46).

## 6  Case study of wavelength references for optical fiber communications

1 Because of fundamental molecular absorptions when light is projected through the absorption cell filled with acetylene gas, the power transmitted through the

cell is distinct at specified wavelengths, allowing accurate references to those wavelengths. Those references can then be used to calibrate instruments for industry.

2 See Gilbert and Swann (2001, p. 2).

3 The rough breakdown of all of the SRM 2517a sales by industry category is 45 percent to manufacturers of test equipment, 30 percent to manufacturers of components, 10 percent to companies providing network systems, and 15 percent to other users – mostly research laboratories – of the SRM. According to Dr Gilbert, a company will typically purchase one SRM 2517a.

4 The data developed for discussion of the outcomes in this case study are based on discussions with Dr Gilbert and several industry experts from Wavelength References, Burleigh Instruments, Corning, Agilent, and Chorum Technologies.

5 The information about the industry-wide coverage of our sample of respondents in industry was provided by NIST.

6 For a discussion of other optoelectronics SRMs, see: http://patapsco.nist.gov/srmcatalog/tables/view_table.cfm?table=207-4.htm

7 Our understanding is that these activities fall under the rubric of R&D, but absent information about how companies classify these activities we refrain from using the policy-sensitive term "R&D."

8 See also the note to Table 6.1.

9 Industry interacts with NIST and stays abreast of the latest developments through direct communication with NIST scientists, and through scientists' presentations and publications. In this case, some respondents reported that they began benefiting from the new knowledge – gained from interaction with NIST researchers – about wavelength calibration even before SRMs were sold as industry coped with the need for the actual SRMs but substituted experimental work in their absence.

10 As is seen in Figure 6.1, in addition to gaining new profits that we have identified as industrial benefits, industry loses some of its previous profits on the previous amount sold before unit costs fell because the use of SRM 2517a lowers costs and consequently price falls. However, those lost profits (lost producer surplus) are completely offset by a gain of exactly that amount in consumer surplus, leaving just the new profits measured in Table 6.3 and represented by $A + B + C$ in Figure 6.1 as the increase in total surplus because of increased producer surplus. The net gain in consumer surplus (represented by $D$ in Figure 6.1) is then added to get the change in total economic surplus that is the social return to the use of SRM 2517a – consumers gain more than $D$, but that additional gain is exactly offset by an equal amount lost from previously existing surplus for producers, leaving $D$ as the net gain in consumer surplus.

11 Note that Figure 6.1 depicts optimal output in the long run when all costs are variable.

## 7 Case study of injectable composite bone grafts

1 Much of this background information came from a face-to-face interview with Dr Wang on October 23, 2001 at NIST, and from subsequent correspondence. Also, Dr Fred Eichmiller, director of the American Dental Association Health Foundation Paffenbarger Research Center at NIST, provided useful information through extensive telephone interviews.

2 Background information on the Paffenbarger Research Center is at www.adahf.org/paffen.html

3  See  http://www.adahf.org/ada/prod/adaf/paffenbarger/prog_bone.asp,  Calcium Phosphate Bone Cement PRC Research Program.

4  This section is based on extensive telephone discussions with Dr Fred Eichmiller of the ADA, Dr John Rendall at the University of North Carolina Medical School, and Mr John Ruesch at the ADA Survey Research Center.

5  Because these interviews were conducted in early and mid-2002, it is assumed that these and other such cost saving estimates reflect costs in 2001.

6  According to the ADA Survey Research Center, there were 640,000 dental implants in 1990 and the growth rate has been over 12 percent per year.

7  According to the ADA Survey Research Center, there were 230,000 osseous grafts in 1990 and a 12 percent annual growth rate was used to project the number in 2001.

8  The 1999 estimate came from the US Department of Health and Human Services, and that number increased at about 30 percent per year during the 1990s. See *Statistical Abstract of the United States, 2001*, Table 168.

9  Several pharmaceutical companies, such as Johnson & Johnson, do market grafting cements. Discussions with marketing representatives from these companies, who in turn said that they discussed our queries with those in corporate R&D, verified that the pharmaceutical industry did not have injectable grafting materials on their near-term research agendas.

10  These individuals did not want to be identified, and neither did the contact person in corporate R&D.


## 8  Case study of Internet commerce for manufacturing

1  Much of this background information came from a face-to-face interview with Mr Rhodes and Ms Goldstein on October 23, 2001 at NIST, and from subsequent correspondence with both of them. During the telephone interviews with industry experts, much of the background information in this section was discussed in an effort to focus the interview.

2  See www.jabil.com

3  See www.rosettanet.org

4  In 1999, the IPC changed its name from Institute of Interconnecting and Packaging Electronic Circuits to IPC. Now, the organization is known as IPC – Association Connecting Electronics Industries. See www.ipc.org

5  See www.nemi.org. Information on the related NEMI FIS is at www.fis.nemi.org

6  See IPC-2571 at http://www.gencam.org

7  By delimiting the evaluation focus of the study to PDX standards we made the study tractable but at the same time delimited the estimable benefits.

8  This section is based on extensive telephone discussions with individuals identified by Mr Rhodes and Ms Goldstein. The recommended contact individuals represent companies throughout the supply chain, including OEMs Lucent, Agilent (spin off from Hewlett Packard), and Intel, and EMSs Sanmina-SCI, Router Solutions, and Teradyne. Individuals from the IPC were also contacted.

9  Those interviewed were, as expected, not familiar with the ICM project at NIST, but they were familiar with the critically important role of those involved in the ICM project during the period of the ICM project.

10  See www.ableco.com

11  This was an interesting observation since part of the motivation for the ICM project was pressure from OEMs to develop such standards.

12 A case could be made that OEM benefits should be forecast for the same length of time as benefits to the EMS industry since the PDX standard affects both parties.

## 9 Case study of polymer composite dielectrics for integrated thin-film capacitors

1 This background information came from a face-to-face interview with Dr Obrzut on October 23, 2001 at NIST and from subsequent correspondence. The technical definitions came from the on-line version of the *McGraw-Hill Encyclopedia of Science & Technology*, accessed through the Dartmouth College Information System.

2 Dielectric material, also known as dielectric, is a material that is an electrical insulator or in which an electric field can be sustained with a minimum dissipation of power. Dielectric film is a film possessing dielectric properties; it is used as the central layer of a capacitor.

3 The embedded capacitance is capacitance placed within the board rather than being attached to its exterior surface. Capacitance is the ratio of the charge on one of the conductors of a capacitor (there being an equal and opposite charge on the other conductor) to the potential difference between the conductors. A capacitor is a device that consists essentially of two conductors (such as parallel metal plates) insulated from each other by a dielectric and that introduces capacitance into a circuit, stores electrical energy, blocks the flow of direct current, and permits the flow of alternating current to a degree dependent on the capacitor's capacitance and the current frequency.

4 Dielectric constant is also known as relative dielectric constant, relative permittivity, and specific inductive capacity. For an isotropic (having identical properties in all directions) medium, dielectric constant is the ratio of the capacitance of a capacitor filled with a given dielectric to that of the same capacitor having only a vacuum as dielectric. Units are rationalized meter-kilogram-second units or centimeter-gram-second electrostatic units. Permittivity is the dielectric constant multiplied by the permittivity of empty space, where the permittivity of empty space is a constant appearing in Coulomb's law and has value of 1 in centimeter-gram-second electrostatic units and value of $8.854 \times 10^{-12}$ F/m in rationalized meter-kilogram-second units.

5 Electrical impedance, also known as complex impedance, is the total opposition that a circuit presents to an alternating current, equal to the complex ratio of the voltage to the current in complex notation.

6 Toward successfully meeting these objectives, the project achieved four technical milestones. First, the research developed a prototype microwave test fixture for dielectric permittivity measurements of films using the APC-7 coaxial test port configuration. APC-7 is the Hewlett Packard (HP) set-up standard; it is good up to high frequencies and provided NIST with the best configuration to work with given the objectives of the research. Second, the research developed computing algorithms suitable for quickly measuring impedance characteristics and transient charging of embedded decoupling capacitors. Third, the research analyzed the high-frequency relaxation process – that has been discovered in high dielectric constant composites – by investigating relaxation behavior of model polymer matrices filled with ferroelectric powders. And fourth, the research led to presentations and publications of the results to reach appropriate audiences.

7  Dielectric loss, also known as dielectric absorption, is the electric energy that is converted into heat in a dielectric subjected to a varying electric field.

8  The ATP intramural project enabled the team to focus on industry's needs as those needs were identified in the ATP Microelectronics Manufacturing Infrastructure Focus Program. For a description of that program, see: http://www.atp.nist.gov/atp/focus/micro.htm

9  A microwave is an electromagnetic wave that has a wavelength between about 0.3 and 30 cm, corresponding to frequencies of 1–100 GHz.

10 The data developed for discussion of the outcomes in this case study are based on discussions with Dr Obrzut at NIST and interviews of several respondents in industry. Special thanks for their time and insights are due to respondents from StorageTek, Merix, DuPont, National Center for Manufacturing Science (NCMS), 3M, Nortel, Gould Electronics, Oak-Mitsui, and Coretec.

11 Paraphrasing one respondent: there are other tests than Dr Obrzut's that are available, but they do not properly characterize the thin dielectric materials. Dr Obrzut's test does properly characterize them.

12 Paraphrasing the observations of another respondent: Dr Obrzut's test method is a good method for the materials suppliers to allow them to do standardized tests and have understanding of the properties of their dielectric materials. The test method is not directly applicable to OEMs because the materials are already laminated into the printed circuit board by the time the OEMs get them. The test will be useful for the board fabricators to verify what they are getting from the materials suppliers. The test is being documented as an IPC standard.

13 Asked about the importance of Dr Obrzut's test, a respondent with an OEM replied: "Without Dr Obrzut's test it would be like going down the freeway without visual. If I ask for a certain dielectric constant, then I expect that to be built into the board when it gets to me. Dr Obrzut's test will allow characterization using a small sample of material and a small sample preparation effort. Without his test, we would not have full knowledge about the material."

14 One respondent observed: "The production/failure costs avoided (increased yields realized) are of course down the road since the embedded capacitance is now only in prototypes. But the printed wiring board manufacturers would have reduced costs because of scrap avoided. In planning a new introduction, when figuring price they figure a factor for anticipated scrap."

An observer of the industry who has been actively involved in the development of embedded passive devices technology observed: "Such savings are going to be there down the road, and already as the materials manufacturers deal with the OEMs making prototypes such savings may be realized."

Another respondent observed: "Without the NIST testing methods, when an OEM found that a board did not behave as expected, a three-way battle would develop among materials suppliers, board fabricators, and OEMs. An OEM could refuse to accept a board."

A materials supplier was asked: now, you do have these new materials, and they are in a small number of test vehicles. Regarding that development of new materials that you have at the moment, what would have happened at your company absent the NIST research outputs? The materials supplier responded: "We would have just continued to charge ahead making the materials. We would have relied on the OEMs to tell us if the materials were behaving properly in the applications. If they had not behaved as expected, we might have thought the problems were design specific. There would have been a lack of ability to really understand the materials' performance. In sum, we would have made the materials anyway, and then relied on the OEMs for performance evaluations." The materials supplier was then asked: Can you put a cost on that; can you quantify the benefits of having the new test metrology in terms of reduced problems of dealing with the OEM and board manufacturers? The response: "No, not yet, because the test is not yet routinely used sufficiently to have data yet. The vision of how it will be beneficial is correct, but we do not yet have dollar benefit data on the actual effects."

15 Paraphrasing the observations of one respondent: the greater flow of communications output enabled by the new embedded capacitance is of course still down the road since only prototypes currently exist of the embedded capacitance. The downturn in the industry has hurt the advancement of implementation of the technology. The larger OEMs would of course be looking at the embedding of capacitance in prototypes, trying to understand the behavior of embedded capacitance. But the design tools needed to put the material into the components are not yet in place. So designers if using the dielectric materials must force-feed the materials through the design process.

Paraphrasing the observations of another respondent, a board fabricator: the benefits of the NIST research output have not really flowed down to us yet. The development of the new standards is underway. The benefit of the NIST research will be the ability to make accurate measurements. The ability to say, make me a material that meets these properties using this test. We'll be buying materials from sources that are required to test in a certain way. As a fabricator, we will have the ability to process these new materials and put them into products for OEMs. The AEPT Consortium [the NCMS Advanced Embedded Passives Technology Consortium] is working to commercialize the new products. The embedded capacitance technology will enable new products. An OEM in the consortium believes that as the specification requirements for performance increase, the thin film embedded capacitance approach is the only way to meet the new requirements. Cost is not the issue, but performance. Some of the work the consortium has done suggests that with embedded resistors and capacitors a 30 percent reduction in board size is possible.

16 The estimate for the in-kind contribution from industry was reported by a knowledgeable person from industry who was actively involved with Dr Obrzut's project as a key representative from industry in the EDC consortium. To make the estimate, the reporting individual discussed the in-kind investments with other prominent, key individuals in industry who had knowledge of Dr Obrzut's project, and together they reached the figure of $1,345,000.

17 One respondent observed: "We are working hard to commercialize the technology. We expect a commercial product – a material – in one year. We are less than a year from saying we have a commercial product. And, we are working with OEMs to explore the applications of the material. The new product must be sold to OEMs, designers, and fabricators. All of the AEPT consortium's work is aimed at accelerating the commercial application of embedded passive technology. The Obrzut/NIST test method is a subset of the overall effort."

18 As explained, the benefit stream used for the metrics is a lower bound for what expected profits would have been to support the investment. Changes in market conditions that were not anticipated at the time of the investments delayed the development and commercial application of embedded passive technology. With the passage of more time and the emergence of the actual electronics applications of embedded capacitance in printed wiring boards, the impact of the ATP intramural funded dielectrics project is expected to be substantial.

## 10 Alternative evaluation templates

1 In the extreme case where industry would not have made the investments at all, there are no private-sector costs avoided, but because the private-sector performance shortfall is complete, all of the traditional Griliches–Mansfield stream of returns to the R&D investments is valued as benefits. In that special case, the Link–Scott approach is identical to the Griliches–Mansfield approach except that it has the advantage of having pointed out that government could do the work more efficiently – in this special case because industry would not do it at all. See Link and Scott (1998, chapter 3) for more details about the counterfactual evaluation method.

2 For example of the application of the spillover evaluation method, see Link and Scott (2001a).

# Bibliography

Arrow, K.J. (1962) "Economic welfare and the allocation of resources for invention," in Universities-National Bureau Committee for Economic Research, *The Rate and Direction of Inventive Activity*, Princeton, NJ: Princeton University Press.

Arrow, K.J. (1963) *Social Choice and Individual Values*, second edition, New Haven, CT and London: Yale University Press.

Audretsch, D.B. (1995) *Innovation and Industry Evolution*, Cambridge, MA: MIT Press.

Baldwin, W.L. and Scott, J.T. (1987) *Market Structure and Technological Change*, London: Harwood Academic Publishers.

Bush, V. (1945) *Science – the Endless Frontier*, Washington, DC: US Government Printing Office.

Council of Economic Advisers (CEA) (1994) *Economic Report of the President*, Washington, DC: US Government Printing Office.

Council of Economic Advisers (CEA) (2000) *Economic Report of the President*, Washington, DC: US Government Printing Office.

Council of Economic Advisers (CEA) (2002) *Economic Report of the President*, Washington, DC: US Government Printing Office.

David, P.A. (1987) "Some new standards for the economics of standardization in the information age," in P. Dasgupta and P. Stoneman (eds), *Economic Policy and Technological Performance*, Cambridge, UK: Cambridge University Press.

Executive Office of the President (EOP) (1990) *U.S. Technology Policy*, Washington, DC: Office of Science and Technology Policy.

Gilbert, S.L. and Swann, W.C. (2001) "Acetylene $^{12}C_2H_2$ absorption reference for 1510 nm to 1540 nm wavelength calibration – SRM 2517a," NIST Special Publication 260–133, Gaithersburg, MD: National Institute of Standards and Technology.

Greene, W.H. *LIMDEP Version 8.0* (within Nlogit 3.0, Version 3.02, November 26, 2002), Plainview, NY: Econometric Software, Inc.

Griliches, Z. (1958) "Research costs and social returns: hybrid corn and related innovations," *Journal of Political Economy*, 66: 419–431.

Hall, B.H., Link, A.N., and Scott, J.T. (2001) "Barriers inhibiting industry from partnering with universities: evidence from the Advanced Technology Program," *Journal of Technology Transfer*, 26: 87–98.

Hall, B.H., Link, A.N., and Scott, J.T. (2003) "Universities as research partners," *The Review of Economics and Statistics*, 85: 485–491.

Jaffe, A.B. (1998) "The importance of 'spillovers' in the policy mission of the ATP," *Journal of Technology Transfer*, 23: 11–19.

Leyden, D.P. and Link, A.N. (1999) "Federal laboratories as research partners," *International Journal of Industrial Organization*, 17: 572–592.

Link, A.N. (1996a) "Economic impact assessment guidelines for conducting and interpreting assessment studies," NIST Planning Report 96–1, Gaithersburg, MD: National Institute of Standards and Technology.

Link, A.N. (1996b) *Evaluating Public Sector Research and Development*, New York: Praeger Publishers.

Link, A.N. (1996c) "On the classification of R&D," *Research Policy*, 25: 379–401.

Link, A.N. (1998) "Public/private partnerships as a tool to support industrial R&D: experiences in the United States," Report prepared for the Working Group on Technology and Innovation Policy, Division of Science and Technology at OECD.

Link, A.N. (1999) "Public/private partnerships in the United States," *Industry and Innovation*, 6: 191–216.

Link, A.N. and Scott, J.T. (1998) *Public Accountability: Evaluating Technology-based Institutions*, Norwell, MA: Kluwer Academic Publishers.

Link, A.N. and Scott, J.T. (2001a) "Public/private partnerships: stimulating competition in a dynamic market," *International Journal of Industrial Organization*, 19: 763–794.

Link, A.N. and Scott, J.T. (2001b) "Economic evaluation of the Baldrige National Quality Program," NIST Planning Report #01–3, Gaithersburg, MD: National Institute of Standards and Technology.

Link, A.N. and Scott, J.T. (2004a) "Evaluation of ATP's intramural research awards program," NIST Report #04–866, Gaithersburg, MD: National Institute of Standards and Technology.

Link, A.N. and Scott, J.T. (2004b) "The role of public research institutions in a national innovation system: an economic perspective," Final Report prepared for The World Bank.

Link, A.N. and Scott, J.T. (2005) "Evaluating public sector R&D programs: the Advanced Technology Program's investment in wavelength references for optical fiber communications," *Journal of Technology Transfer*, 30: 241–251.

Link, A.N. and Scott, J.T. (forthcoming) "An economic evaluation of the Baldrige National Quality Program," *Economics of Innovation and New Technology*.

Mansfield, E., Rapoport, J., Romeo, A., Wagner, S., and Beardsley, G. (1977) "Social and private rates of return from industrial innovations," *Quarterly Journal of Economics*, 91: 221–240.

Martin, S. and Scott, J.T. (2000) "The nature of innovation market failure and the design of public support for private innovation," *Research Policy*, 29: 437–447.

Nelson, R.R. (ed.) (1993) *National Innovation Systems: A Comparative Analysis*, New York: Oxford University Press.

Office of Management and Budget (1992) "Circular No. A-94: guidelines and discount rates for benefit-cost analysis of federal programs," Washington, DC.

Office of Management and Budget (1996) "Economic analysis of federal regulations under Executive Order 12866," Washington, DC.

Office of Science and Technology Policy (OSTP) (1994) "Science in the national interest," Washington, DC: Executive Office of the President.

Office of Science and Technology Policy (OSTP) (1998) "Science and technology: shaping the twenty-first century," Washington, DC: Executive Office of the President.

Ruegg, R. and Feller, I. (2003) "A toolkit for evaluating public R&D investment models, methods, and findings from ATP's first decade," NIST Report #03–857, Gaithersburg, MD: National Institute of Standards and Technology.

Scott, J.T. (1998) "Financing and leveraging public/private partnerships: the hurdle-lowering auction," *STI (Science, Technology, Industry) Review*, 23: 67–84.

StataCorp (2001) *Stata Statistical Software: Release 7.0*, College Station, TX: Stata Corporation.

Tassey, G. (1992) *Technology Infrastructure and Competitive Position*, Norwell, MA: Kluwer Academic Publishers.

Tassey, G. (1997) *The Economics of R&D Policy*, Westport, CT: Quorum Books.

Tassey, G. (2003) "Methods for assessing the economic impacts of government R&D," NIST Planning Report #03–01, Gaithersburg, MD: National Institute of Standards and Technology.

Tassey, G. (2005) "Underinvestment in public good technologies," *Journal of Technology Transfer*, 30: 89–113.

Teece, D.J. (1980) "Economies of scope and the scope of the enterprise," *Journal of Economic Behavior and Organization*, 1: 223–247.

Teece, D.J. (2005) "Technology and technology transfer: Mansfieldian inspirations and subsequent developments," *Journal of Technology Transfer*, 30: 17–33.

U.S. Census Bureau (2002) *Statistical Abstract of the United States, 2001*, Washington, DC: US Government Printing Office.

# Index

3M 114; C-Ply 97

Acts: American Technology
    Preeminence 1; Omnibus Trade and
    Competitiveness 1
ADA see American Dental
    Association
ADAHF see American Dental
    Association Health Foundation
Advanced Embedded Passives
    Technology (AEPT)
    Consortium 115
Advanced Technology Program (ATP)
    17; framework of intramural
    research awards program 7–8;
    intramural research program 3;
    Microelectronics Manufacturing
    Infrastructure Focus Program 114;
    NIST projects funded by 28;
    projects supported by 29
Advanced Technology Program (ATP)
    intramural funding: effect in
    achieving similar goals and
    milestones 48; probability
    of undertaking similar research
    project absent 46, 48;
    quantitative analysis of effects of
    27, 42–43, 108–109
Agilent 111–112
American Dental Association (ADA)
    81, 111–112
American Dental Association Health
    Foundation (ADAHF), Paffenbarger
    Research Center (PRC) 81, 111
American Technology Preeminence Act
    see Acts

APC-7 coaxial test 113
Arrow, K.J. 11, 17, 107–108;
    definition of innovation 107
ATP see Advanced Technology
    Program
Audretsch, D.B. 18

Baldwin, W.L. 15
barriers to innovation and technology
    13–16
benefit data 67
benefit-to-cost ratio see project
BFRL see Building and Fire Research
    Laboratory
bone graft material 81–82
BoneSource® 81
Building and Fire Research Laboratory
    (BFRL) 5, 91
Burleigh Instruments 111
Bush, President G. 10
Bush, V. 110
business-to-business (B2B) electronic
    commerce (e-commerce) 88

Calcium Phosphate Bone Cement
    PRC Research Program 112
calcium phosphate cement 81
capacitors 113; integrated
    thin-film 95, 113
case studies: candidate intramural
    research projects for 65; initial
    candidate intramural research
    projects for 64; injectable
    composite bone grafts 81–87,
    111–112; Internet Commerce for
    Manufacturing (ICM) 88–94, 112;

case studies (*Continued*)
  optical fiber communications
    70–80; polymer composite
    dielectrics 95–102; selection and
    methodology 63–6, 109–110
Chemical Science and Technology
  Laboratory (CSTL) 5
chemistry and life sciences (CLS) 63
Chorum Technologies 111
citations 37–8
Clinton, President W. 10–11
Competency awards 43
complex impedance *see* electrical
  impedance
consumer surplus 67
Cooperative Research and
  Development Agreement (CRADA)
  27, 42
Coretec 114
Corning 111
Coulomb's law 113
Council of Economic Advisers
  (CEA) 110
counterfactual evaluation method
  103–4
CRADA *see* Cooperative Research and
  Development Agreement

Dartmouth College Information
  System 113
David, P.A. 108
dental or orthopaedic surgeries 81
dielectric absorption *see* dielectric loss
dielectric constant 113
dielectric films 96–97, 113
dielectric loss 114
dielectric permittivity
  measurements 113
diffusion of advances from research 19
Digital Cordless Standard 96
DuPont 114; HiK 97

e-commerce *see* electronic commerce
economic analysis *see* economic
  evaluation of publicly funded
  research
Economic Assessment Office (EAO) 2
economic evaluation of publicly
  funded research 24, 77–80, 87, 94,
  101–102, 110

*Economic Report of the President*:
  1994 10; 2000 11, 68
EEEL *see* Electronics and Electrical
  Engineering Laboratory
Eichmiller, F. 83, 85, 112
electrical impedance 113
electronic commerce 88; for
  manufacturing 91
Electronics and Electrical Engineering
  Laboratory (EEEL) 4, 89, 91;
  Optical Fiber and Components
  Group 70, 77; Optoelectronics
  Division 77
electronics and photonics technology
  (EPT) 63
electronics manufacturing services
  (EMS): cost savings 92;
  EMS-to-supplier interface 91;
  industry 88
embedded capacitance 95, 113
Embedded Decoupling Capacitance
  (EDC) Industrial Consortium
  97, 99
evaluation: of public R&D investments
  106; studies sponsored by the
  Program Office at NIST 110;
  systematic methodology 66–67;
  templates, alternative 103, 116;
  *see also* economic evaluation of
  publicly funded research
evaluation methods: counterfactual
  103–104; Griliches and
  Mansfield 67, 103, 116;
  spillover 104–105, 116

Feller, I. 106

GenCAM (IPC 2510) 89–90
generic technology 106
Gilbert, S.L. 70–72, 75, 111
Goldstein, B. 88–90, 112
Gould Electronics 114
Government Performance and Results
  Act (GPRA), United States
  109–110
government role in supporting
  innovation 10, 66
Greene, W.H. 109; full information
  maximum likelihood approach 37
Griliches, Z. 66, 103

Griliches and Mansfield evaluation
  method 67, 103, 116
GSM Global System for Mobile
  Communications 96

HADCO EmCap 97
Hall, B.H. 19
Heckman model 37, 50
Hewlett Packard 88

ICM *see* Internet Commerce for
  Manufacturing (ICM) case study
iDEN Integrated Digital Enh.
  Network 96
information technology (IT) 63
Information Technology Laboratory
  (ITL) 5, 89, 91
injectable composite bone grafts, case
  study 82, 111–112; background
  information and overview of the
  project 81; benefit and cost
  information 83–86; cost of dental
  implants 83; estimated total costs
  and estimated total social benefits
  associated with 86; implications for
  industry and society 82–83;
  orthopaedic procedures on joints to
  become closed procedures 84;
  recovery time from orthopaedic
  surgeries 84; results of
  economic analysis 87; social
  benefits 85; success rate of
  periodontal surgeries 83
innovation: government role in
  supporting 10, 66; investment
  in, private and social rates of return
  to 67; and technology, barriers
  to 13–16
Institute of Interconnecting and
  Packaging Electronic Circuits 112
Intel 88, 112
intellectual property rights 15
internal rate of return (IRR)
  *see* project
Internet Commerce for Manufacturing
  (ICM) case study 88–90, 112–113;
  background information and
  overview of project 88; benefit
  and cost information 92–94;
  estimated total costs and estimated

total social benefits associated with
  93; evaluation metrics for 94;
  implications for industry and
  society 90–91; results of economic
  analysis 94
intramural research: allocation of funds
  4–7; awards 2; hypothetical effects
  of funding 46–62
IPC 90, 112; dielectric test standard,
  new 98; *see also* Product Data
  eXchange, standards
ITL *see* Information Technology
  Laboratory

Jaffe, A.B. 12

knowledge spillovers 42

laboratory research, effect of ATP
  intramural funding on scope of 31
leveraging additional funding 42
Leyden, D.P. 108
Link, A.N. 17, 101, 106–108,
  110, 116
Link–Scott approach 116
Lucent Technologies 88, 112

*McGraw Hill Encyclopedia of
  Science & Technology* 113
Malcolm Baldrige National Quality
  Award Program 108
Mansfield, E. 66, 103
Manufacturing Engineering Laboratory
  (MEL) 4, 89, 91
Manufacturing Extension Partnership
  (MEP) Program 88, 91
market entry, cost of 15
market failure 10–13, 66; theory of
  public policies to address 107
Martin, S. 11, 17
Materials Science and Engineering
  Laboratory (MSEL) 5; Polymers
  Division 81, 95
Measurement and Standards
  Laboratories (MSLs) 1, 3
MEL *see* Manufacturing Engineering
  Laboratory
MEP *see* Manufacturing Extension
  Partnership
Merix 114

metrology for electrical properties of
    embedded capacitance 95
micro-spheres 82
microwave 114; packaging 96;
    prototype test fixture for dielectric
    permittivity measurements 113
Motorola 88
MSLs *see* Measurement and Standards
    Laboratories

National Center for Manufacturing
    Science (NCMS) 114; Advanced
    Embedded Passives Technology
    Consortium 115
National Electronics Manufacturing
    Initiative (NEMI): Technology
    Roadmap 89; Virtual Factory
    Information Interchange Project
    (VFIIP) 89
National Institute of Dental and
    Craniofacial Research (NIDCR)
    81–82
National Institute of Health (NIH) 81
National Institute of Standards and
    Technology (NIST): benchmarks 28,
    43–45; laboratory structure at 3–7;
    National Advanced Manufacturing
    Testbed (NAMT) project 91;
    research laboratories 4, 63
National Science Foundation reporting
    category of R&D spending 106
NCMS *see* National Center for
    Manufacturing Science
NEMI *see* National Electronics
    Manufacturing Initiative
net present value (NPV) *see* project
NIDCR *see* National Institute of
    Dental and Craniofacial Research
NIST *see* National Institute of
    Standards and Technology
Nortel 114

Oak-Mitsui 114
Obrzut, J. 95, 97–100, 113–115
OEMs *see* original equipment
    manufacturers
Office of Inspector General (OIG), US
    Department of Commerce report 2
Office of Management and Budget
    69, 107

Omnibus Trade and Competitiveness
    Act *see* Acts
Optical Fiber and Components Group
    *see* Electronics and Electrical
    Engineering Laboratory
optical fiber communications, case
    study 71; benefit and cost
    information 72–77; calibration cost
    savings 74; estimated costs
    associated with SRM 2517a 77;
    increased production yields 74;
    industry and society implications for
    71–72; industry benefits 76;
    industry benefits associated with
    SRM 2517a 78; negotiations cost
    savings 74–75; production related
    engineering and experimentation cost
    savings 73; reduced marketing costs
    75; results of economic analysis
    77–80; *see also* SRM 2517a
Optoelectronics Division *see*
    Electronics and Electrical
    Engineering Laboratory
original equipment manufacturers
    (OEMs) 88–89; cost savings 92

Paffenbarger Research Center *see*
    American Dental Association
    Health Foundation
patents 38; from ATP intramural
    projects 40
path dependency 15
PDX *see* Product Data eXchange
periodontal surgeries 83
Physics Laboratory (PL) 5
PI survey instrument 22–24; response
    rates to 29–31
polymer composite dielectrics for
    integrated thin-film capacitors case
    study 95, 113; background
    information and overview of the
    project 95–96, 113; benefit and
    cost information 98–101;
    benefit-to-cost ratio 67–69;
    enabling new products 99;
    estimated total costs and social
    benefits associated with developed
    test method 100; evaluation metrics
    for 101; implications for industry
    and society 96–97; materials

characterization savings 98;
net present value (NPV) 67–69;
production yield increases and
negotiation cost savings 99; results
of economic analysis 101–102
Polymers Division *see* Materials
Science and Engineering
Laboratory
presentations 38–42; from ATP
intramural projects 40
printed circuit boards (PCBs) 88
private hurdle rate 107
Product Data eXchange (PDX) 90;
standards 91–93, 113
project: databases, new 58, 62;
duration of 56, 60; internal rate of
return (IRR) 67–69; measurement
technology, new 57, 61; outputs
and outcomes 31–43; related
research 59; scope 52–54, 60;
standards, new 58, 61; technical
challenge in 54–55, 60; technical
papers from 57, 61
publications 33–37; for ATP
intramural and NIST projects
34, 45
public funding: and private
performance of research, spillovers
model in 105; R&D investments,
evaluation of 106
public-good nature of research focus 66
public research institutions, role of 10,
17–21, 107–108

quantitative analysis of effects of
ATP intramural funding 27,
108–109

R&D: barriers to innovation and
technology 13–16; cooperative
efforts 18–19; investment costs
15; of private firms 104–105;
public investments, evaluation of
106; social and private rates of
return to 12; spending, National
Science Foundation reporting
category of 106; spillover
gap in 12; underinvestment in
11–13
Rendall, Dr J. 112

research: basic 19; objectives of
government 20
Rhodes, T. 88–90, 112
RosettaNet 89
Router Solutions 112
Ruegg, R. 106
Ruesch, Mr J. 112

Sanmina-SCI 112
schedule for projects, work ahead of
49–52
*Science and Technology, Shaping the
Twenty-First Century* (OSTP)
10–11
*Science in the National Interest* 10
Scott, J.T. 11, 15, 17, 101, 107–108,
110, 116
selection process of intramural
research projects for case study
63–66
social benefits from innovation 67
social hurdle rate 107
social rate of return metrics 67–69
Software Diagnostics and
Conformance Testing Division of
ITL 88
spillover evaluation method
104–105, 116
spillover gap in R&D 12
SRM 2517a 111; cells 75; industry
benefits associated with 78;
related research of Optical Fiber
and Components Group 71;
technology 73
Standard Reference Data 106
Standard reference material
(SRM) 70–71, 106; *see also*
SRM 2517a
StorageTek 114
Supply Chain (B2B) Communication
of Quantity Product Data 89
survey instrument for NIST PIs
22–24
Swann, W.C. 71, 111

Tassey, G. 12, 17, 106, 108
technical risk 14
technology: complexity of 16; with
high science content 19; lock-in 15;
transfer 18

*Technology Services* 106
Teradyne 112

University of North Carolina Medical
   School 112
US Department of Health and Human
   Services 112
US Government Performance and
   Results Act (GPRA) of 1993 104
*US Technology Policy* 1990 10

Wang, F. 81–83, 85–86, 111;
   intramural project 81

wavelength: calibration standard 71;
   references for optical fiber
   communications, case study of
   110–111
wavelength division multiplexed
   (WDM), optical fiber
   communications
   systems 70
Wavelength References 111
Web-based data sharing 89
wiring boards 95

XML 91